PALEO SLOW COOKER

Learn How to Live Healthier and Lose Weight Rapidly

(Healthy Gluten-free Recipes Made Easy)

Milton Holden

Published by Sharon Lohan

© **Milton Holden**

All Rights Reserved

Paleo Slow Cooker: Learn How to Live Healthier and Lose Weight Rapidly (Healthy Gluten-free Recipes Made Easy)

ISBN 978-1-990334-11-5

All rights reserved. No part of this guide may be reproduced in any form without permission in writing from the publisher except in the case of brief quotations embodied in critical articles or reviews.

Legal & Disclaimer

The information contained in this book is not designed to replace or take the place of any form of medicine or professional medical advice. The information in this book has been provided for educational and entertainment purposes only.

The information contained in this book has been compiled from sources deemed reliable, and it is accurate to the best of the Author's knowledge; however, the Author cannot guarantee its accuracy and validity and cannot be held liable for any errors or omissions. Changes are periodically made to this book. You must consult your doctor or get professional medical advice before using any of the suggested remedies, techniques, or information in this book.

Table of contents

Part 1 1

Introduction 2

Chapter 1 - Making a Perfect Pitch for the Paleo Diet .. 3

Chapter 2 - Knowing What Is And What Is Not Paleo . 14

Chapter 3 - The Crockpot to the Rescue 20

Chapter 4 - If it is Paleo, It must be Gluten-Free 31

Chapter 5 - The Top 50 Easy Paleo Slow Cooker Recipes 34

Crockpot Paleo Pulled Pork Chili Ingredients 34

#2 Hawaiian Paleo Pizza Salad 36

#3 Pork Short Rib Breakfast Tacos (Boneless) 39

#5 Blueberry Bacon with Maple Breakfast Carnitas ... 43

#6 Crockpot Sweet Potato Basil Soup 46

#7 Easy Shredded Pork w/ Caramelized Mashed Plantains 49

- #8 Easy Crockpot Breakfast Pie 51
- #9 Marinated Asian Crockpot Beef Spare Ribs 53
- #10 Crockpot Short Ribs Coffee Ancho Chile.............. 54
- #11 Brazilian Curry Chicken Crockpot Style 56
- #12 Ropa Vieja with Cuban Style Rice 59
- #13 Slow Cooked Rump Roast w/ Mushroom Gravy .. 62
- #14 Shredded Pork w/ Honey, Apple & Ginger 64
- #15 Enchilada Chicken Stew.. 65
- #16 Garlic Pork and Cauliflower Rice 68
- #17 Crockpot Beef & Mushroom Stew........................ 70
- #18 Paleo Pork Green Chile Crockpot 71
- #19 Crockpot Bacon-Wrapped Chicken...................... 74
- #20 Slow-Cooked Pork Ribs.. 75
- #21 CHICKEN MUSAKHAN CROCKPOT......................... 76
- #22 Crockpot Puerco Pibil 78
- #23 Apple Pork Tenderloin... 80

#24 Cranapple Turkey Breast 82

#25 Greek Inspired Stuffed Chicken Breasts............... 83

#26 Paleo Crockpot Jambalaya Soup......................... 85

#27 Easy Crockpot Lamb Roast 89

#28 Crockpot Kimchi Chicken..................................... 90

#29 Crockpot Beef Tongue w/ Roasted Pepper Sauce 92

#30 Classic Corned Beef and Cabbage....................... 94

#31 Slow Cooked Buffalo Chicken Meatballs 96

#32 Sweet &Savory Sage Stew w/ Pumpkin and Cherries 98

#33 Crockpot Pepper Steak – Asian Version............. 100

#34 Pork Lettuce Wraps – Asian Twist 101

#35 Mexican Pulled Chicken Stuffed Peppers 103

#36 Crockpot BOEUF BOURGUIGNON....................... 105

#37 Crockpot Italian Meat Balls 108

#38 Paleo Braised Beef Shanks 109

#39 Salsa Pork Chops 110

#40 Lamb Ribs Curry w/ Sweet Onions and Fresh Garlic 112

#41 Cambodian Lime Ginger & Honey Ribs 113

#42 Paleo Crockpot Fudge 115

#43 Paleo Crab Chili Chowder 117

#44 Paleo Orange Chicken 119

#45 Crockpot Stuffed Cabbage Rolls 121

#46 Dijon Brussel Sprouts with Bacon Ends 124

#47 Acorn Squash Stuffed with Cinnamon, Apple, and Turkey 125

#48 COFFEE BRAISED BEEF CHILE 126

#49 Crockpot Chicken Stroganoff 128

#50 Slow Cooker Chicken Cacciatore 129

Chapter 6 - Frequently Asked Questions about Slow Cookers 131

Conclusion 137

Part 2 138

Crockpot Pulled Pork Chili 138

Slow Cooker Paleo BBQ Brisket Recipe 140

Paleo Slow Cooker Oxtail Stew Recipe 142

Homemade Thai Chicken Broth 144

Slow Cooker Paleo Jerk Chicken 146

Slow Cooker Bacon & Chicken 148

Paleo Ropa Vieja Recipe 150

Slow Cooked Corned Beef Brisket and Roasted Cabbage 152

Slow Cooker Lemongrass Coconut Chicken Drumsticks 155

Slow Cooker Beef Stew with Cranberries and Rosemary 157

Slow Cooker Beef Stroganoff 159

Crockpot Thai Beef Stew 161

Slow Cooker Squeaky Clean Boeuf Bourgignon 164

Slow-Cooker Beef Brisket With Bourbon BBQ Sauce 166

Roast Stew Paleo 168

Slow Cooker Paleo Meatballs 170

Paleo Crockpot Shredded Beef 171

Hearty Crock Pot Chili Stew 174

5-Spice Slow-Cooker Pork Ribs 176

Easy Barbecue Slow Cooker Ribs 179

Slow Cooker Pulled Pork 181

Slow Cooker Chinese Spare Ribs 184

Conclusion 187

Part 1

Introduction

This book contains all there is to know about the Paleo Diet, including the top 50 easy-to-follow Paleo Slow Cooker Recipes for those who wish to adopt the Paleo lifestyle for the first time. This book will guide you on how to easily adapt and prepare popular recipes the Paleo diet way. The book also explains why the Paleo Diet is more than just an eating regimen. It is more of a lifestyle that encompasses almost all the dietary principles upon which all other dietary regimens (including the gluten-free diet) are founded. Most important of all, it shares with you the easiest way to convert traditional dishes into Paleo using the slow cooker.

For those who are thinking of embracing the Paleo concept for the first time, this book is specifically designed for you. It has a wealth of useful information on how to prepare healthy Paleo dishes with ease through the set-and-forget method of slow cooking - the Paleo way.

Thanks again for downloading this book. I hope you enjoy it!

Chapter 1 - Making a Perfect Pitch for the Paleo Diet

The Paleo Diet has remained the most searched for key phrases in the "diets" category on Google, indicating the continuing interest for this diet dubbed as the next big thing (*the last big thing for some*) in health and nutrition. The term Paleo Diet was coined by Dr. Loren Cordain, who wrote a book about the primal diet with the same title. Dr. Cordain is an acknowledged expert in the evolutionary basis of diet and diseases having over 100 peer-reviewed scientific abstracts and articles on the subject. The book *The Paleo Diet,* first published in 2002, gave birth to the Paleo movement, which promoted the diet and recognized Dr. Cordain as its erstwhile leader and founder.

Advocates of the movement adhere to the primal way of eating as espoused by Dr. Cordain in his book. The Paleo Diet, as Dr. Cordain called it, is actually more than just an ordinary eating regimen. It is more of a lifestyle that promotes health and fitness. It involves adopting the eating habits of our primal ancestors from the prehistoric era to the stone-age (Paleolithic) and Neolithic eras. This is the period before man discovered and nurtured the knowledge and the skill of raising and growing his own food (Agriculture). The diet is about eating food in its most natural state possible - similar to what our primal ancestors had been consuming for millions of years.

The Paleo Diet is built on the premise that most of what ails man today is because of what he eats today – a premise that is shared not only by Dr. Cordain (whose past and present research works centered on the anthropological and evolutionary origins of modern man's diet, well-being, and health) but also by Dr. David Perlmutter who is a neurologist with many awards, and an internationally acclaimed leader in the study of nutritional influences leading to neurological disorders, particularly in regards to how wheat damages our brains and wreaks havoc on our bodies.

The Primal Diet has become embedded in the Human Genome

Based on anthropological evidence, it is believed that the earliest primates from whom modern man evolved subsisted on a diet made up of fruits, plants, and insects for 60 million years. When he learned how to fashion tools and weapons from stone and discovered how to make fire about 2.6 million years ago, he became more than a gatherer foraging for food. He became a hunter as well hunting down wild animals to eat. (*This was the stone-age era or the Paleolithic era. The word 'Paleolithic' is derived from two Greek words which mean "Old age of the stone" or Stone Age for short.*)

It was also the era when man learned how to use fire for the first time to cook the meat from the wild animals he hunted down. During this era, wild meat became part of his diet in addition to the fruits and plants he was able to forage from the wild. These prehistoric men subsisted on minimally processed natural food for millions of years, and the human body was thought to have adapted to it perfectly - so much so that the human genome (DNA) is believed to have been programmed already to source his nutritional requirements from minimally processed natural food sources having been used to eating wild plants, fruits, and animals for over 62 million years.

However, the advent of agriculture and the development of animal husbandry just a little over 10,000 years ago drastically overhauled the food intake of people almost instantaneously. Grains like wheat, rye and barley, which were easy to grow in large quantities and can be stored far longer than any other food item, were produced on a large scale and soon became the staple, replacing the traditional minimally processed natural food sources of man altogether.

The sudden changeover to a new diet was fueled further by the ensuing industrial revolution, which created groundbreaking technology, which allowed food manufacturers to process food large scale. Processed food found a home among the growing population whose hectic lifestyle in a fast-paced, highly industrialized society robbed precious time needed to prepare fresh food. Mass production of processed food soon became the norm, matched by an unprecedented wholesale consumption by people whose food choices have by now changed to cope with their busy schedules. They now prefer processed foodstuff to natural and slightly processed food to which the human body has been programmed to source its nutrient requirements millions of years ago.

With the drastic changes in the human diet taking place so suddenly, nutrition and health experts began to theorize that the shift from natural food sources to bulk produced crops and processed food products have created a discordance between our naturally evolved ancient human genome resulting in varied bodily reactions, leading to the development of diseases in modern times.

Researchers believe 10,000 years is not long enough to change what it took the body millions of years to program into the human genome. They theorized that forcing the human body to adapt to bulk-produced crops and modern processed foods caused it to be naturally strained. They have in fact compiled voluminous proof showing that this discordance is what caused many of the illnesses of modern times. Their conclusion: the human body has not fully adapted to contemporary foodstuff.

What exactly did our Paleolithic Ancestor Eat?

Admittedly, it would be hard to pinpoint exactly what our primal ancestors actually ate during their era in as much as historical accounts were simply non- existent then. We only know that the type of food prehistoric people ate was largely limited to what was available in their geographic locations at any given time. However, by using the numerous laboratory analyses made on newly dug up prehistoric bones of Paleolithic people, it is quite clear that the diet was high in protein, low in carbohydrate, and rich in beneficial fats. We can attempt to replicate a semblance of the primal diet through a logical process of eliminating the type of food we consume today, which could not have possibly been consumed by our primal ancestors during their time. At least, we can come up with an educated guess and a good approximation of what might have constituted the primal diet.

For example:

- They could not have consumed dairy products then, since animals were wild and undomesticated then. It would be wishful thinking to assume that they were able to milk wild cows or other wild animals as this would put them in grave danger.

- He did not learn how to grow plants until only *a little over 10,000 years ago*, so we can safely assume cereal grains were never a staple like they are today. They may have consumed grains, but they would be limited to what they were able to gather from the grass that grew wild in the fields.

Salt was a stranger to them too. There is no evidence showing our primal ancestors were mining salt during their era. The most they could have done then to get a salty taste in their food was to dip their food in salt water. But then again, this would be limited to those living along or near the seashores.

- Sugar is a modern concoction and could not have possibly been a part of their diet. To sweeten their food, they may have gone for natural sources of sugar like wild honey, which incidentally was also quite difficult to find at that time.

- Lean meat from wild animals was their ordinary fare, which means their diet had more protein content than today's diets.

- Their carbohydrate intake came from non-starchy wild fruits and plants, which are rich in fiber but low in calories as compared to modern diets.

- For fats, they had healthy omega3 fats, polyunsaturated fats and monounsaturated fats, which are all heart-friendly as they come from fresh fish and lean meat from the wild. Saturated fats and trans-fats, which are industrially produced and are eternally present in today's processed foods that regularly decorate our dining tables were absolutely non-existent then.

So what constitutes the Primal Diet?

It would be safe to assume that the primal diet our prehistoric ancestors consumed for millions of years before agriculture changed it almost overnight consisted mainly of lean meat from free-ranging, grass feeding wild animals, non-starchy wild fruits, nuts, vegetables that are low in carbohydrates, fish, and seafood that is rich in heart friendly omega 3 fats. It is basically a diet that is high in protein, low in carbohydrate, and has low calorie content.

Researchers who have long been investigating the primal diet have also noticed an important observation worth pursuing – the significant absence of chronic illnesses and diseases that ail man today among our pre-historic ancestors. They noted that prehistoric men didn't suffer from such health conditions like cardiovascular disease, cancer, diabetes, gout, osteoporosis, varicose veins, macular degeneration, autoimmune diseases, glaucoma, all of which afflict modern man. This leads researchers to believe that the phenomenon must be related to the food he eats.

Apart from Dr. Lorain Cordain and Dr. David Perlmutter, there were other known researchers before and after them whose various research collectively leads to one commonsensical conclusion: the typical, largely grain-based, sugar-loaded contemporary Western Diet is the root cause of the modern diseases we've just enumerated above. This is not a mere conjecture or an unfounded theory but a well-supported fact complete with verified research works and clinical studies to back it up. This is a nasty reality that food manufacturers (*who are more concerned with the profit they make than the health and well-being of the consumers*) have been trying to keep under wraps.

Contemporary Western Diet altered our Normal Nutritional Intake

The normal nutrient intake of the human body, which sustained man for millions of years and to which the human genome had perfectly adapted, has been significantly altered by modern food sources. For example, the usual protein content of contemporary diets is only 15% while the body is used to having an average of 19% to 35% protein from the primal diet.

One significant change from the traditional primal diet is that contemporary diets rely heavily on grains and refined sugar as the main source of carbohydrates for energy. Sadly however, grains and sugar have high glycemic loads and can raise the blood sugar levels a whole lot more than the non-starchy fruits, nuts and vegetables, which used to be the main sources of carbohydrates of our stone-age ancestors.

Several studies have exposed the sad truth about the standard American diet (SAD) – it uses sugars and cereals to supply 39% of the body's energy needs. These same studies revealed that the glycemic indexes of both sugar and grains are high enough to induce spikes in blood sugar levels. They contain simple sugars that are easily absorbed by our system. Health experts have continuously linked the Standard American Diet (SAD) to the high incidence of chronic diseases affecting a large number of Americans today. Despite the many revealing studies about SAD, we continue to live in a society where the food manufacturers and producers are seemingly unconcerned about our health and where health authorities pay little attention to the food we eat.

Just look at some of the statistics below and you will understand what we mean.

- 65% of adults in the U.S. aged 20 and above are either obese or at least overweight.

- More than 64 million Americans suffer from a form of cardiovascular disease.

- Another 50 million suffer from hypertension. 11 million Americans have type 2 diabetes, which results from having high concentrations of sugar in blood plasma over an extended period of time.

- There are studies showing that 25% of deaths in the country are due to cancer and a third of these deaths are caused by nutritional factors.

To make the story short – what ails modern man is in the food he eats. The type of food we eat today is high in sugar and genetically modified grains. Man never had this kind of diet 200 years ago. Unfortunately, as people warmed up to this modern diet, the incidence of chronic diseases and illnesses dramatically rose too in tandem with the increased consumption of the sugar-loaded and grain dominated modern diet. Apparently, people with weaker immune systems started developing negative reactions that led to the high incidence of chronic illnesses and diseases.

Chapter 2 - Knowing What Is And What Is Not Paleo

The Paleo Diet is not a mere dietary regimen but a whole new lifestyle that is all about eating clean. It is about supplying the body with food that it has been genetically programmed to thrive on. It is about steering away from those foods that skew the body's hormonal balance and put the immune system in a disruptive state of disarray and confusion. It is about helping the body attain its optimal performance by basically putting a stop to the onslaught of toxic garbage that comes from processed and bulk-produced food into our system. It is about giving the liver a break from being continuously pre-occupied with ridding the body of all the toxic garbage you used to eat daily.

The Paleo Diet is basically about eating food in its most natural state possible while eliminating food that can potentially wreak havoc on the body. This means if you wish to understand Paleo better, you must first be familiar with *what is* and *what is not* Paleo. Before you can adapt the lifestyle, you need to know by heart what food groups are not in the Paleo food list or those that must be eliminated from the Paleo diet.

Below is a list of **food groups that should not be on your Paleo shopping list** together with an explanation of why they have been excluded, aside from the fact that most of them were non-existent during the Paleolithic era.

- **Grains, Corn, and Soy**

Wheat, Barley, Corn, Rice, Millet, Oats, (including products derived from them like bread, pasta, couscous, biscuits, cereals and cakes)

All beans, Lentils, Chickpeas, Peas, Peanuts and all products derived from soybeans like soya milk, soy sauce, and tofu

Most of the foods under this group are genetically modified to be resistant to pest and pesticides and to produce higher yields. They therefore contain *transgenes* as well as fertilizer and pesticide and herbicide residues that can be transferred to our systems when we consume these products or any of the products derived from them.

They also contain enzyme inhibitors and other anti nutrients, such as *Obesogens* or chemical compounds that are foreign to the body and disrupt the endocrine system wreaking havoc on the normal course of development of lipids and balance metabolism causing one to become obese or overweight; Lectins which interfere with the body's metabolic activities, disrupt insulin functions, and prevent absorption of nutrients; Phytates which binds nutrients preventing them from being absorbed by the body; and gluten which causes irritation and inflammation of the intestinal wall.

- **Dairy Products**

    Milk, Yoghurt, Cheese, Butter, etc

    It is not only because dairy products could not have been consumed by our primal ancestors because they were non-existent then that dairy products are considered as non-Paleo. It is also because dairy products contain lactose and casein - two substances that usually cause severe immune reaction and allergies among many of us. On top of that, the milk that is used to make the dairy products comes from ranch-raised cows, which are normally injected with rBGH or Bovine Growth Hormone and fed with genetically modified corn meal or Alfalfa. These are transferred to our bodies through the dairy products we eat.

- **Sugar**

Refined sugar, raw or brown sugar, molasses, sugar cane, sugar containing candies and confectioneries

Sugar has no nutritional value at all except for being a source of carbohydrates for energy. It does however have a high glycemic load that can cause frequent spikes in the blood sugar levels since it can be absorbed into the bloodstreams easily.

- **Legumes and Beans**

    Lentils, pinto beans, chickpeas, kidney beans, soybeans, broad beans, and peanuts.

    All of these also contain all the anti-nutrients that are found in grains. They are also starchy, which means they are high in quick-release carbohydrates, which can cause spikes in the levels of blood sugar.

- **Potatoes**

    All potatoes except sweet potatoes

They are starchy foods that contain simple sugars that are easily absorbed into our system. They may also contain *Solanine,* a glycol-alkaloid toxin that irritates the gastro-intestinal tract and cause gastro-enteritis.

- **Processed Food**

All Kinds

All processed foods are normally high in sodium, refined sugar, and other food preservatives and additives. Most of them are either produced from or contain genetically modified food and ingredients.

- **Transfat and other highly processed oils**

They have been shown to raise the levels of bad cholesterol (LDL) in the blood at the same time lower the level of good cholesterol (HDL).

Food Groups that should be on your Paleo Shopping List

- *Lean meat* from pasture-raised, certified-organic, grass-fed livestock or from wild game animals. If in case grass-fed, organic meat is unavailable, you can buy lean meat instead and avoid the fat. The toxins in these animals are likely to be in their fat, the same way humans store the toxins in their fat cells. The lean meat choices may be choice cuts from Beef, Pork, Chicken, Duck, Turkey, and Lamb. Game meat could be from wild deer, wild boar, buffalo, pheasant, as well as exotic meat like crocodile meat.

Fish and seafood caught from the wild like Tuna, Trout, Salmon, Sardines, Mackerel, Mussels, Bream, Crab, Monkfish, Sea bass, Prawns, and more. You should avoid those that have been raised in fish pens, as they are likely to be fed with fishmeal produced from genetically modified crops. Fish and seafood raised in fish pens have unusually high mercury levels too.

- *Nuts and Seeds* like Almonds, Walnuts Brazil Nuts, Hazelnuts, and seeds like Sesame seeds, Pumpkin seeds, and Sunflower seeds. They have high protein content and contain beneficial fats like Omega 3.

- *Beneficial Oils* like organic extra virgin coconut oil, pork bacon fat from pasture-raised cows, butter or ghee from grass-fed cows, extra virgin almond oil, and extra virgin olive oil.

Fruits and Vegetables

– organically grown and not genetically modified, free from insecticides, herbicides, and fertilizer residues, and have not been irradiated. This includes all certified organic farm produce.

Chapter 3 - The Crockpot to the Rescue

Most people who go on a diet or follow a dietary regimen for whatever reason always find themselves quitting the diet altogether after some time. According to a study made by a UK-based company, 2 out of 5 quit within the first week. 1 out of 5 make it to the end of the month. Only 20% actually make it to the third month. We can't expect it to be any different for those who would like to go Paleo. In fact, it may even be worse because the Paleo diet is not just like any other weight loss diet. It is a lifestyle that you will have to adopt for the rest of your life. It will require preparing Paleo meals every single day, which could be quite a change to one who has a very hectic lifestyle. It could enslave you for the rest of your life to the kitchen.

That is of course if you have not discovered yet the magic of slow cookers, more popularly known as the 'Crockpot'. The crock is the most under-rated cooking tool in your kitchen where it is probably gathering dust. I can't blame you because like most others you probably think that the slow cooker is merely for *'making stews and tenderizing tough meat cuts'*. That was its traditional role in the kitchen until just recently when people began to rediscover the many benefits of a slow cooker, particularly among those who hardly have kitchen time after coming home exhausted from working the whole day. But since people are getting conscious about the kind of food they put into their bodies, they have started warming up to the idea of slow cooking and preparing meals ahead of time so they can come home with a ready, healthy, hot meal waiting to be served. And guess what, these people started replacing microwave ovens with crockpots, and discarding TV dinners and fast foods for home-cooked healthy meals.

The crockpot offers the most plausible solution to the busy moms' dilemma. It offers easy and quick ways to prepare delicious and healthy dinners without having to spend hours in the kitchen. The 'set-and forget' feature of the slow cooker is simply suited to today's hectic lifestyle. There is also a remarkable array of sumptuous and healthy meals that can be prepared using the crockpot all of which require very minimal preparation. Dinner can be served within minutes after you come home from work. Best of all, changing over to a healthy Paleo lifestyle would be a breeze instead of a struggle if you use the slow cooker to prepare Paleo meals for the whole family.

Using the crockpot is simple and straightforward. You simply fill it up with your pre-cut and pre-prepared ingredients, set the timer and the temperature setting (*high or low*) to the desired setting, and leave it to do its magic while you attend to other things like going to work.

You may in fact even prepare all the ingredients for the next whole week's meals on one lazy weekend and just freeze them for future use. Then every night before going to bed, you simply choose what dinner you want for the next day and thaw it overnight. Before going to work the next day, you simply plop the thawed ingredients into the crockpot. Presto; when you come home from work, you will have a hot, healthy dinner waiting to be served. For breakfast, simply plop in a pre-prepared Paleo breakfast meal straight from the freezer into the crockpot and let it cook while you sleep.

'Crockpot' is actually a popular brand of a slow cooker. It is so popular that it became a familiar kitchen fixture in millions of American homes. It is so common that the name Crockpot became synonymous with slow cookers. When you mention slow cooker, the first thing that crops up in people's minds nowadays is "Crockpot" and vice versa.

How the Crockpot Came To Be

The crockpot that we know today originated from the Naxon Beanery, an all-purpose cooking appliance that produces an *'old world oven'* effect invented by aircraft engineer and talented inventor Irving Naxon. He called it the Naxon Beanery.

Naxon later sold the Naxon Beanery to Rival Manufacturing where one of its employees Robert J. Scott modified it by making a new ceramic insert to serve as the 'crock'. They had it patented in 1974 and called it the Crockpot. Since then, the Crockpot has found its way to millions of American kitchens. Its popularity however started to dim when processed TV dinners came onto the scene, followed on its heels by the microwave ovens. Both offered unmatched convenience and hassle-free preparations, which were more than perfect for the busy working moms.

The Crockpot was relegated to the sidelines and used sparingly - only for *'making stews and tenderizing tough meat cuts'*. They were kept on the kitchen cupboards most of the time to gather dust – but not for long. The negative effects of highly processed food and TV dinners started creeping into the people's' consciousness. People were starting to become aware of the detrimental effects of the grain-dominated and sugar and sodium-loaded processed food. They have also become wary of the ill effects of the microwave oven radiation on their health. They also have become extra careful of what they put in their mouths.

People's preference for food started to shift away from processed foods slowly favoring healthier, more natural food sources and thrusting junk foods, fast foods, and all other highly processed foods aside. The only bottleneck remaining is the busy moms' hectic schedule. It is still the breadwinner moms who have to endure the heat of an oven top as well as the long hours spent on preparing dinner for the family. With 40% of married woman being 'bread winner' moms (*and that does not include the single working moms yet*), the problem is not something that can be shrugged off that easily.

Of course, these breadwinner moms have difficulty juggling their time to prepare hot dinners for the families and still have moments for their own needs. No matter how exhausted they may be from the day's grind, they still can't escape from their cooking chores to feed their hungry brood. The temptation to buy fast food or junk processed food to quench the family's hunger pangs can be overwhelming and irresistible.

It is a good thing someone invented the slow cooker, which today is like a breath of fresh air for the busy breadwinner moms. The slow cooker is turning out to be the busy mom's best friend rescuing her finally from being a lifetime slave to her kitchen chores.

Here are the Benefits of a Crockpot

You get to choose the healthy ingredients for your meals.

In contrast to packaged and processed foods where you have no choice but to accept whatever it is in the package, with crockpot cooking you get to choose the healthy ingredients according to the recipe of your choice. Besides, you get to use only the most nutritious ingredients mainly from fresh farm produce. You get to cook the meals at low temperatures over a long period of time preventing the nutrients from being lost while retaining the juices inside the slow cooker.

Slow Cooker Saves a Great Deal of Time and Effort

For most slow cooker recipes, you need only to plop in all the pre-prepared ngredients and let it do its magic. It's a simple 'set and forget' operation. No need to spend hours in front of a hot stove while cooking a meal. All it requires is a little time to prepare the ingredients, which is something you can even do long before the actual cooking. Unlike cooking on an oven top where you have to watch what you are cooking to avoid scorching or overcooking, with the Crockpot you simply set it and come back after the cooking time is done. It saves you enough time to attend to your own personal needs. You can even go to work without ever worrying about what may happen to your cooking at home.

Energy Efficient and Truly Economical

The crockpot uses less energy than a conventional electric oven or an oven top, which means you get to save a lot in electric bills. It also doesn't make the kitchen hotter like an oven top and therefore you don't use as much heating fuel as you normally would when using an oven top.

The slow cooker is ideal for busy families who would love to come home to a hot, hearty meal after a long day at work without the need to spend a lot of time preparing the food. You may have to get up a bit earlier than usual to prepare the meat, spices and vegetables to throw into the crockpot before you leave it cooking and go to work. And you need not worry about running out of cooking ideas because there are lots of recipes that are available online that can be prepared in your crockpot, from the standard casseroles and stews, to soups, and puddings, and even mulled wine. You could also make curry and chili. You can even use two slow cookers and have the main dish cooking in one while the side dish or dessert is cooking in the other.

If you've kept your slow cooker aside for a long time to gather dust in a cupboard, it is high time to get it out, clean it and start looking for some slow cooker recipes in line with the Paleo lifestyle. It will make your life easier...and healthier.

Here are some more tips on how to use your slow cooker properly

1. The slow cooker has two temperature settings – the High (*with temperature at approximately 300^0 F*) and the Low (*with temperature at approximately 200^0 F*).

2. Before use, make sure you preheat the slow cooker for a few minutes before adding your ingredients.

3. One hour of cooking on high temperature setting is equivalent to two hours to two and a half hours cooking on low.

4. Whenever you can, brown the meat prior to placing it in the crockpot to make sure the juice is retained in the meat. You also have to make sure the liquids

are boiling before you add the meat. This will improve the texture and flavor of the meat.

5. Never lift or open the lid while cooking. Opening the lid even briefly will add 15 to 20 minutes to the cooking time because it will take that much time to recover the lost heat and return to its previous temperature.

6. Keep your slow cooker clean at all times. You can soak the pot after each use to remove burnt bits sticking on the sides and bottom of the pot. They may get into your next dish if you don't clean the pot. This is a no-brainer!

7. When chopping vegetables, chop them in small, equal sizes so that they will easily cook through. You also have to make sure the vegetables are covered by the liquid. If you have time, you may also sauté vegetables first before adding them into the slow cooker. Sautéing will improve the flavor of the vegetables.

8. Never add tender vegetables such as tomatoes, mushrooms, and zucchinis at the start of your cooking because they will be over-cooked. Add them only during the last hour of cooking.

9. Never use the slow cooker for reheating leftovers. It will take a long time to get the food piping hot. Use the microwave instead.

10. Don't fill your slow cooker more than 3/4 of the pot because the food won't cook properly. There has to be enough space left for heat to circulate to ensure even cooking.

11. Thaw frozen meat and poultry properly before plopping them into the slow cooker. Never add frozen vegetables too.

12. When putting the ingredients into the crockpot, you should always put the meat and the vegetables first. Any food at the bottom of the crockpot tends to cook faster than the food on top. There is just one exception: the root vegetables should always be under the meat because they cook slower.

13. When making casserole, curry or chili, prepare them in large batches. Use some now and freeze the rest for later use, especially on days when you come home late from work.

14. Don't add more liquid than what the recipe calls for. Slow cooking creates more liquid while cooking. Adding more may spoil the taste.

15. If after cooking a casserole it is still too watery, you can take the lid off and run the slow cooker on high. Cook for half an hour with the lid off or until the casserole is no longer watery.

16. Don't prepare meal ingredients in the slow cooker pot and place it inside the refrigerator overnight ready for slow cooking the next morning. This will chill the pot, thus lengthening the cooking time.

17. Never used ground or powdered seasonings. They lose their flavor and aroma during prolonged cooking. Instead, use fresh whole herbs or leaves. If you have no choice but to use ground seasonings, then try to add them only during the last hour of your cooking.

18. Cut down large chunks of meats and trim excess fat so that pieces will easily fit into your slow cooker. You must also remove the skin of any poultry products before putting them into the slow cooker. Trimming meat fat and removing poultry skin will minimize the excess fat that will result from prolonged cooking.

19. Consider garnishing the meals before serving to make them more visually appealing. Simply add tomato slices, chopped red pepper, parsley, chives,

or cheese. Take note that prolonged cooking will fade the color of your food, making it look a lot less appealing.

Chapter 4 - If it is Paleo, It must be Gluten-Free

Another kind of diet that has gained a lot of attention in the past few years is the gluten-free diet. You must already be familiar with it since entertainment news has continuously featured a lot of famous celebrities endorsing the diet for weight loss. Among them is Miley Cyrus who even exhorted her fans to follow suit. Undeniably, these celebrity endorsers have lost a lot of weight as can be gleaned from their photos showing their slim and trim figures. This fast rising fad diet has seemingly and erroneously been equated to good health and weight loss as a result.

We can't help but make a comparison between the Paleo Diet and the gluten-free diet since people would naturally want to know the difference. First of all, the gluten-free diet is a medically prescribed diet designed specifically for people suffering from celiac disease and those with gluten sensitivity. However, because of the numerous celebrity endorsements, even non-sufferers began to warm up to the gluten-free diet giving birth to a new, multi-million dollar gluten-free food industry.

But, it is not really surprising to see non-sufferers experience some remarkable results with the diets because like the Paleo Diet, it shoots down wheat, which is one of the staples of the standard American diet that is being linked to the high incidence of chronic diseases of modern man.

If you are familiar with the gluten free diet, the first thing you will notice are key similarities between these two diets – they both eliminate wheat, barley, and rye and everything else that has gluten in it from the diet plans. This key similarity alone is what made these two diets so effective and popular that both were able to develop a legion of loyal followers.

Since the Paleo diet eliminates all types of grains from its list (especially gluten-loaded wheat, barley and rye), the primal diet is essentially gluten free. It might interest you to know however that if the Paleo Diet is gluten-free, not everything that is gluten-free is Paleo.

The real difference between a Paleo diet and the gluten-free diet is in the kinds of foods that are eliminated from the respective diets.

With the gluten-free diet, wheat, barley, rye, triticale, and everything else that has gluten in it are eliminated from the diet plan. With the Paleo diet, you eliminate not only the gluten-loaded grains, but all grains in general which are genetically modified. It also eliminates dairy products.

The Paleo Diet is founded on whole foods similar to those our primal ancestors would have eaten. These foods are healthy and nutritious because they are free from artificial additives, genetic modification, and chemical residues that most processed foods contain.

On the other hand, the gluten-free diet being primarily designed out of a medical necessity is merely focused on eliminating all possible sources of gluten. People who adapt to the diet by choice think that it is a healthier alternative to the standard American diet. Unfortunately, this is only true as far as eliminating grains like wheat, barley, and rye.

When gluten-free diets become so popular, food manufacturers saw an opportunity to make a killing and started producing 'gluten-free' products. Sadly however, many of these products are not 100% gluten-free since the FDA allowed products with no more than 25 parts per billion of gluten to be labeled gluten-free. On top of that, the gluten-free diet allows the inclusion of processed gluten-free foods, which are loaded with sugar, heavy in trans-fats, and use artificial ingredients.

Many people who go gluten-free by choice do not realize the danger they are still exposed to.

Therefore, the best way to go gluten-free without making a mistake at all is to adapt the Paleo lifestyle instead. The Paleo Diet is both gluten-free and all natural. Of course, we are not discounting the other option of following an all-natural gluten-free diet and avoiding processed foods altogether, but the simplest way is to go Paleo and prepare your own Paleo gluten-free meals.

Chapter 5 - The Top 50 Easy Paleo Slow Cooker Recipes

Crockpot Paleo Pulled Pork Chili

Ingredients

2 lbs pork roast (trim excess fat)

3 cloves of garlic, (be sure they are peeled)

3 tbsp paprika, smoked

½ cup hot sauce

2 tbsp garlic powder

1 tbsp cumin

2 tbsp chili powder

Salt

1 tbsp red pepper flakes

2 tsp cayenne pepper

2 diced yellow onions

1 diced red bell pepper

1 diced yellow bell pepper

2 cans of tomatoes, fire roasted (14 oz each)

1 can of tomato sauce (14 oz)   Avocado   slices   (for garnishing)

Diced green onions, (for garnishing)

Instructions

- Set the pork roast at the bottom of your crockpot.

- Thrust the point of a knife into the pork roast in 3 different spots to make 3 holes. Press the garlic cloves deep into the holes.

- Pour the hot sauce evenly over the top of the roast.

- Sprinkle the top with garlic powder, paprika, chili powder, cayenne pepper, cumin, salt, and red pepper flakes on top of the roast.

- Put the diced onions, tomatoes, tomato sauce, and peppers on top of the meat.

- Put on the lid and slow cook with low setting for 8 to 10 hours.

- If desired, garnish with green onions together with sliced avocado before serving.

Makes 6 to 8 servings

#2 Hawaiian Paleo Pizza Salad

Ingredients

For the garlic crockpot pork:

2 to 3 lb pork shoulder (bone-in)

4 cloves of peeled garlic

1 yellow onion, sliced

1 tsp garlic powder

Salt to taste

For the salad:

Romaine lettuce, 2 hearts, chopped roughly

1 diced red bell pepper, core taken out

1 can (4 oz) button mushrooms, sliced

2 cups pineapple, diced

½ cup pepperoni, diced

2 tbsp coconut oil

Instructions

- Layout the onion slices at the bottom of the crockpot then put the pork shoulder on top of them.

- Thrust a sharp knife into the pork shoulder in 4 different places making 4 different holes.

- Insert each of the garlic cloves into each hole and press each one in. Sprinkle the pork shoulder and onions with salt and garlic powder.

- Put on the crock-pot cover and cook for 8 to 10 hours on low.

- Once the cooking is done, shred the cooked pork shoulder directly in the slow cooker.

Once your meat is shredded, it is time to prepare the rest of

the salad.

- Heat 2 tablespoons of coconut oil in a medium size skillet over medium to high heat, then add the mushrooms with a pinch of salt and cook until brown and soft.

- Add the cooked mushrooms with all the other ingredients.

- Place on a serving dish and top with any dressing you desire.

#3 Pork Short Rib Breakfast Tacos (Boneless)

Ingredients

For the "tortillas"

3 eggs, whisked

½ C coconut milk

2 tbsp garlic powder

2 tbsp chili powder

1 tbsp cumin

Pinch of salt

For the shredded pork

2 lbs pork short ribs, boneless

2 tbsp maple syrup

2 tsp garlic powder

Salt, to taste

For the toppings

5 to 6 bacon strips

1 can green chile (6-8 oz)

2 to 3 tbsp hot sauce

Chopped green onions

Instructions

- Place the pork short ribs into the crockpot. Pour the 2 tbsp maple syrup on top of the ribs, along with 2 tbsp of garlic powder and one pinch of salt.

- Set the cooker on low and cook for 8 to 10 hours.

- When done cooking, take the pork ribs out of the crockpot and shred them using two forks. Drench the shredded pork with some of the juice from the crockpot for extra flavor.

- To make the tortillas, whisk all the tortilla ingredients together in a medium size bowl until smooth.

- Now heat a large non-stick skillet (medium to high heat) and pour in the enough tortilla mixture to make tortilla the size of a pancake size. Roll the skillet around while cooking to flatten out the tortilla evenly. Cook each side for just one minute.

- Once all the tortillas are done (about 8 to 10 tortillas), place the bacon strips on the skillet and cook them crisp on both sides. Cool and chop roughly.

- Mix the hot sauce and the green chile together in a bowl and place in microwave to heat for one and a half to two minutes then chop the green chile.

- Load each of the tortillas with shredded pork, bacon, green chile, and green onions.

#4 Short Rib Maple Bacon Burgers With Mustard

Ingredients

For short ribs

1.5 cups Maple Mustard Sauce (Paleo Variety)

4 lbs Beef Short Ribs

Half a cup broth (beef or chicken will do)   Mince

2 cloves of garlic

Pinch of pepper

Pinch of salt

For burgers

Mince 2 cloves of garlic

1.5 lbs Ground Beef

Salt & pepper

Half a yellow onion, chopped

Around 8 pieces of bacon

More Maple Mustard Sauce for burger topping

Instructions

- Put the beef short ribs inside the slow cooker. Pour in the chicken or beef broth to the slow cooker.

- Cover the ribs with the mustard sauce. Add the minced garlic and sprinkle with salt and pepper.

- Set the temperature on low and slow cook for 8 to 10 hours.

- Place the bacon slices on a baking sheet and place inside the oven preheated to 4050. Cook until the bacon pieces are crispy (about 10 to 12 minutes).

- Shred the cooked beef short ribs in another bowl using a fork. Drain excess fat.

- Place all the burger ingredients together in a bowl and mix until well blended.

- Form the mixture into regular size burger patties.

- Use a large skillet to cook the burger patties over medium to high heat. Cook each side for 4 to 5 minutes. Do not overcrowd the skillets with too many patties. You can do it in batches.

- Place one cooked bacon slice on top of each of the burger patties and pour a little maple mustard sauce on top.

- Serve with some greens if you wish.

Makes 7 burgers

#5 Blueberry Bacon with Maple Breakfast Carnitas

Ingredients

2-3 lbs pork roast (shoulder)

2 cups blueberries

¼ cup maple syrup

½ tsp dried sage

1 tsp dried parsley

1 teaspoon cinnamon

¼ tsp nutmeg

Salt

black pepper

½ cup apple juice

fresh chopped parsley (for garnishing)

4 to 5 bacon strips

Instructions

- Place the pork roast inside the crockpot.

- Add in the one half cup apple juice.

- Pour the ¼ cup maple syrup on the meat and then add a pinch of salt and pepper, 1 teaspoon cinnamon, 1 tsp dried parsley, ½ tsp dried sage and ¼ tsp nutmeg on top of the pork roast. Top off the pork roast with 2 cups blueberries.

- Put the cover on and set the temperature on low. Cook for around 8 hours.

- After 8 hours remove the pork roast and shred using a fork. Drench the shredded pork roast with the remaining juice in the crockpot to keep it moist and retain its flavor.

- In a pan, cook the strips of bacon until crisp. Place them on a plate covered with paper towel to cool. Roughly chop the bacon strips. Afterwards remove most of the rendered fat from the pan leaving behind just a little.

- Take half of the chopped bacon pieces and mix them with the shredded pork roast.

- Put some bacon fat on a pan and place over medium to high heat. Using your hands form balls of the shredded bacon and pork mixture and press each one down to form a patty. Place the patties in the hot pan and press down some more using a spatula. Cook each side for about 3 to 4 minutes before flipping.

• Place the carnitas on a serving plate and top with fresh chopped parsley and the remaining chopped bacon.

#6 Crockpot Sweet Potato Basil Soup

Ingredients

1 coconut milk can (14oz)

½ sliced yellow onion

2 yams or sweet potatoes, diced

1 cup vegetable broth

1 tbsp basil, dried

2 cloves of garlic, minced

salt

Pepper

Instructions

- Place all the listed ingredients inside the slow cooker (in no particular order).

- Mix a little and cover.

- Set the temperature on high and cook for three hours.

- Puree the cooked mixture using a hand blender, or food processor until the whole mixture is smoothly blended.

- You may add some leftover meat to the soup if you wish.

Preparation time 5 min

Cooking time 3 hours

Total processing time 3 hours 5 min

Makes 3 to 4 servings

#7 Easy Shredded Pork w/ Caramelized Mashed Plantains

Ingredients

For the crock pot pork

2 lb pork loin

1 yellow onion, sliced

5 cups beef broth (no added sugar)

1 tbsp garlic powder

1 tsp onion powder

salt and pepper

For the plantain mash

4 brown plantains, sliced lengthwise in half

2 tbsp coconut oil

3-4 tbsp coconut milk

pinch of salt

Instructions

- Add all the listed pork ingredients to the crockpot. Set the temperature on low and cook for 8 to 10 hours.

- Remove the pork loin after cooking and shred it using two forks.

- Heat 2 tbsp coconut oil in a large skillet over medium heat. Once the oil is hot add the plantain slices.

- Dash with salt and some cinnamon.

- Cook each side until soft (about 4 to 5 minutes).

- Place the plantain slices in a food processor and puree. Pour 3 to 4 tablespoons of coconut oil while the food processor is running and continue to puree until you get a smooth mixture.

- Place a blob of the plantain mash to a serving plate and top with shredded pork loin. Top with avocado slices.

Preparation time 10 min

Cooking time 10 hours

Total processing time 10 hours 10 min

Makes 4 to 6 servings

#8 Easy Crockpot Breakfast Pie

Ingredients

8 eggs, whisked

1 sweet potato

1 lb Pork Sausage, diced

1 diced yellow onion

1 tbsp garlic powder

2 tsp dried basil

salt

pepper

Instructions

- Grease all sides of a slow cooker with a little coconut oil to prevent the egg from sticking to the surface.

- Shred the sweet potato with a grater or with a food processor with a shredding attachment.

- Now add all the listed ingredients including the shredded sweet potato into the slow cooker.

- Mix with a spoon to combine.

- Cover and set the temperature on low and cook for 6 to 8 hours.

- To make sure the pork sausage is completely cooked make it at least 7 hours.

- Slice it the way you would slice a pie.

Preparation time 10 min

Cooking time 8 hours

Total processing time 8 hours 10 min

Makes 4 to 6 servings

#9 Marinated Asian Crockpot Beef Spare Ribs

Ingredients

4-6 lbs Beef Short Ribs

Juice from 1 lime

3 tbsp Coconut Aminos

2 tbsp white wine vinegar

1 tbsp raw honey

1 tbsp sesame oil

2 tsp grated ginger, fresh

1 tsp siracha

2 tsp sesame seeds

Instructions

- Place the beef short ribs in a large shallow dish (or baking dish).

- Place the remaining ingredients (except the pork ribs) together in a separate bowl and mix to make the marinade.

- Pour all of this marinade over the beef short ribs.

- Cover and marinate inside the refrigerator for at least 8 hours.

- After at least 8 hours, place the marinated ribs in a slow cooker.

- Pour remaining marinade on top.

- Cover and set the temperature on low and cook for 6 to 8 hours or until meat starts to fall from the bone.

Preparation time 10 min

Cooking time 7 hours

Total processing time 7 hours 10 min

Makes 2 to 4 servings

#10 Crockpot Short Ribs Coffee Ancho Chile

Ingredients

4 lbs Beef Short Ribs

1 cup of brewed coffee (your choice)

1 yellow onion, large, roughly sliced

4 ancho chile, dried, stem less & seedless

4 cloves of garlic

2 tbsp raw honey

2 tbsp olive oil, extra virgin

1 tbsp lime juice

½ cup water or vegetable broth salt

pepper

Instructions

- Place the dried ancho chile in a bowl and submerge in hot water until soft (around 20 to 30 minutes).

- Add the softened ancho chile, together with 1 cup brewed coffee, 4 cloves of garlic cloves, 2 tbsp raw honey, 2 tbsp olive oil, 1 tbsp limejuice in a food processor and add some pepper and salt. Puree into a smooth sauce.

- Place the roughly sliced onions at the bottom of your slow cooker and add ½ cup of water (or vegetable broth).

- Stack the beef short ribs on top of the sliced onions then pour the coffee-ancho chile mixture all over them.

- Add a bit of salt to suit your taste.

- Cover and set the temperature on low and cook for 6 to 8 hours (5 to 7 hours on high).

Preparation time 30 min

Cooking time 8 hours

Total processing time 8 hours 30 min

Makes 3 to 4 servings

#11 Brazilian Curry Chicken Crockpot Style

Ingredients

1.5 to 2 lbs chicken breasts

¾ cup coconut milk

1 cup chicken broth

2 tbsp tomato paste

3 cloves of garlic, minced

1 tbsp ground ginger

4-6 tbsp curry powder

2 chopped bell peppers (1" cubes)

1 thinly sliced yellow onion,

1 dash red pepper flakes

salt

pepper

Instructions

- Place the ¾ cup coconut milk, 2 tbsp of tomato paste, 3 cloves of minced garlic, 1 tbsp ground ginger, 4 to 6 tbsp of curry powder, some salt and pepper, a dash of red pepper flakes into the slow cooker and whisk together.

- Add in chopped bell peppers and the sliced onions.

- Next, add in the chicken then pour 1 cup of chicken broth over the chicken breasts.

- Mix the ingredients until the chicken breasts are fully covered with the curry mixture.

- Cover and set the temperature on low and cook for 6 to 8 hours (4 to 5 hours).

Preparation time 10 min

Cooking time 8 hours

Total processing time 8 hours 10 min

Makes 6 to 8 servings

#12 Ropa Vieja with Cuban Style Rice

Ingredients

For the Ropa Vieja

1 ½ to 2 lbs chuck roast

1 yellow onion

1 red bell pepper

1 yellow bell pepper

1 can tomato sauce

(6 oz) 1 can diced tomatoes (14 oz)

3 tbsp capers, drained

1 tbsp cumin

1 tbsp dried thyme1 tbsp dried oregano

4 cloves of garlic, peeled

1 bay leaf

Salt   Pepper

For the Cuban rice

1 head roughly chopped cauliflower,

(stem removed)

3 thick bacon slices

1 can tomato sauce

(4 oz) 2 tsp cumin

1 tsp garlic powder

1 tsp onion powder

Salt

Pepper

Instructions

- Place the thinly sliced yellow onion and the red and yellow bell pepper slices at the bottom of the slow cooker.
- Plop in the chuck roast on top. Make 4 deep cuts in 4 different places on your chuck roast. Insert and press deeply one garlic clove into each of these cuts.

- Add in all the other spices, including the salt and pepper. Next, pour in 1 can of tomato sauce followed by 1 can of diced tomatoes, 3 tbsp capers, and 1 bay leaf.

- Cover and set the temperature on low. Cook for 6 to 8 hours (5 to 7 hours on high).

Prepare the cauliflower rice

- Chop one head of cauliflower and place the chopped pieces in a food processor with the shredding attachment. Pulse the cauliflower until it has the consistency of rice.

- Place the diced bacon bits on a large saucepan and cook until browned and almost completely cooked through.

- Add the cauliflower rice, 1 can of tomato sauce and all the listed spices to the saucepan. Mix and cover.

- Cook the cauliflower rice while stirring occasionally for 10 to 12 minutes until all the distinct flavors have been incorporated.

- Meanwhile, shred the beef in the slow cooker using two forks.

- Top each serving of Cuban cauliflower rice with the ropa vieja from the crockpot.

Preparation time 10 min

Cooking time 8 hours

Total processing time 8 hours 10 min

Makes 6 to 8 servings

#13 Slow Cooked Rump Roast w/ Mushroom Gravy

Ingredients

1 to 2 pounds beef rump roast

3-4 cups chicken broth

1-2 roughly chopped large onions

5-6 cloves of peeled garlic

1 can of mushrooms, sliced

1 tsp garlic powder

1 tsp onion powder

½ teaspoon paprika

½ cup coconut milk, full-fat, canned

salt & pepper

Instructions

- Place 3 to 4 cups of chicken broth, ½ cup coconut milk, 1 to 2 roughly chopped large onions, 1 tsp garlic powder, 1 can of sliced mushrooms, and the listed spices into your slow cooker and mix together.
- Plop in the beef rump roast placing it in the middle of the mushroom mix.
- Cover your slow cooker and set the temperature on low. Cook for 6 to 8 hours (4 to 6 hours on high).

Preparation time 5 min

Cooking time 8 hours

Total processing time 8 hours 5 min

Makes 4 to 6 servings

#14 Shredded Pork w/ Honey, Apple & Ginger

Ingredients

2 pounds pork shoulder roast

1 sliced yellow onion,

2 sliced apples, cored

⅔ cup beef broth

1 tbsp raw honey

2 tbsp ginger, freshly grated

1 tsp cinnamon

1 tsp salt

½ tsp smoked paprika

½ tsp pepper

2 cloves of garlic, peeled, smashed

1 bay leaf

Instructions

- Place 2/3 cup of beef broth followed by the yellow onions, then the pork shoulder roast, the apple slices, 2 garlic cloves, all the listed spices and 1 bay leaf into the crockpot.

- Cover and set the temperature on low. Cook for 8 to 10 hours (6 to 8 hours on high.

- Shred the pork roast using two forks and serve drenched with some juice from the slow cooker.

Preparation time 5 min

Cooking time 8 hours

Total processing time 8 hours 5 min

Makes 6 to 8 servings

#15 Enchilada Chicken Stew

Ingredients

2 lbs chicken breasts

1 chopped yellow onion

1 chopped green bell pepper

1 can chopped jalapenos (4oz)

1 can chopped green chile (4oz)

2 tbsp coconut oil

1 can diced tomatoes (14oz)

1 can tomato sauce

(7 oz)

3 cloves of garlic, minced

1 tbsp cumin

1 tbsp chili powder

2 tsp dried oregano

salt

pepper

Cilantro for garnishing

Avocado slices for garnishing

Instructions

1. Place the chicken breasts in a slow cooker

2. Add all of the other listed ingredients on top of the chicken breasts in no particular order.

3. Cover and set the temperature on low. Cook for 8 to 10 hours (6 to 8 hours on high).

4. Once the cooking is done, shred the chicken using two forks and combine with the ingredients inside the slow cooker.

5. Top with some avocado slices and cilantro before serving.

Preparation time 10 min

Cooking time 8 hours

Total processing time 8 hours 10 min

Makes 4 to 6 servings

#16 Garlic Pork and Cauliflower Rice

Ingredients

2 lb fat trimmed pork rump roast   Peel

6 garlic cloves

2 head roughly chopped cauliflower, stem & leaves removed

1 C chicken broth

1 tsp ground cumin

1 tsp salt

½ tsp pepper

Instructions

- To make the cauliflower rice, chop the 2 heads of cauliflower and them in a food processor with a shredding attachment. Pulse the cauliflower until it has rice-like consistency.

- Plop the cauliflower rice into the slow cooker together with 1 cup of chicken broth.

- Add 1 tsp ground cumin and 1 tsp salt plus ½ tsp pepper to the cauliflower rice together with 3 garlic cloves.

- Thrust a sharp knife 1" deep in 3 different parts of the pork rump roast then press one garlic clove into each cut.

- Now place the pork rump roast in the slow cooker atop the cauliflower rice.

- Cover and set the temperature on low. Cook for 8 to 10 hours.

- Once done, shred the pork rump roast and mix with cauliflower rice!

Preparation time 6 min

Cooking time 9 hours

Total processing time 9 hours 6 min

Makes 6 to 8 servings

#17 Crockpot Beef & Mushroom Stew

Ingredients

1.5 to 2 lbs beef stew meat   Slice

1 pack of button mushrooms

1 pack shiitake mushrooms, whole

1 pack baby portobello mushrooms

1 chopped sweet potato Peel and smash

4 cloves of garlic

1 cup pearl onions, peeled

1 cup chicken broth (or water)

⅓ cup balsamic vinegar

2 tbsp red wine vinegar

1 bay leaf

2 tbsp onion powder

1 tbsp dried rosemary

1 tsp dried sage

1 tsp dried parsley

salt & pepper

Instructions

- Place all the baby Portobello mushrooms, along with the smashed garlic, and 1 cup of pearl onions at the bottom of a slow cooker.

- Plop in the beef stew meat and the chopped sweet potato on top.

- Add the remaining ingredients putting all of the spices on top of the beef stew meat and the chopped sweet potato. This way the meat juices will ooze down into the Portobello mushrooms. The sweet potatoes won't get too mushy since all the wet ingredients are placed below. Cover and set the temperature on low and cook for 6 to 8 hours.

#18 Paleo Pork Green Chile Crockpot

Ingredients

2 lbs pork roast

1 chopped yellow onion

2 cloves of garlic, minced

3 can green chile (4 oz), diced

2 chopped Anaheim chile (remove seeds)

1 chopped polio pepper, (removed seeds)

1-2 diced jalapeño peppers

2 cups chicken broth

1 can diced tomatoes (8oz)

1 tsp oregano

1 tsp salt

1 tsp white pepper

½ tsp cumin

½ tsp sage

½ tsp paprika

½ tsp cayenne pepper

Instructions

- Place the pork roast at the bottom of the slow cooker and arrange all the vegetables around it.

- Pour all 3 cans of green chile plus 1 can of diced tomatoes all over the pork.

- Scatter all the spices on top.

- Pour 2 cups of chicken broth into the slow cooker.

- Cover the slow cooker and set the temperature on low. Cook for 6 to 8 hours.

- Once cooking is done, use two forks to shred the pork roast. Mix the shredded pork with all the other ingredients before serving.

#19 Crockpot Bacon-Wrapped Chicken

Ingredients

1 ½ cups BBQ sauce, preferably homemade

4 chicken breasts, boneless and skinless

2 tbsp. fresh lemon juice

1 onion, diced

4 peeled apples, chopped

8 - 12 bacon slices

Instructions

- Wrap each of the chicken breasts with the bacon slices.

- Arrange the bacon-wrapped chicken breasts in a slow cooker.

- Combine the home made barbecue sauce, with 2 tbsp of fresh lemon juice, the apple slices, and diced onion in a bowl and mix.

- Pour this barbecue sauce mixture all over the bacon wrapped chicken breasts.

- Cover and set the temperature on low. Cook for 6 to 8 hours.

- Top the chicken breasts with the apple and onion mixture from the slow cooker and serve.

#20 Slow-Cooked Pork Ribs

Ingredients

3 lbs pork spare ribs

3/4 cup water or homemade stock

5 tbsp homemade ketchup

2 tbsp Worcestershire sauce

2 tbsp apple cider vinegar

1 tsp mustard powder;

Sea salt

freshly ground black pepper

Instructions

- Place all the listed ingredients except the pork spare ribs in a slow cooker.

- Mix the ingredients thoroughly to make sure the sauce will be consistent all throughout.

- Place the pork spare ribs in the slow cooker and rub them thoroughly with the sauce making sure it is well coated.

- Cover the slow cooker and set the temperature on low. Cook for 8 hours.

Serve the pork ribs using the cooking liquid for the sauce.

#21 CHICKEN MUSAKHAN CROCKPOT

Ingredients

2 1/2 lbs chicken thighs, boneless, skinless

2 onions, thinly sliced

1 1/2 tbsp olive oil

1/2 oz ground sumac

1 tsp cinnamon

1/4 tsp allspice powder

1/4 tsp cloves, ground

A pinch of saffron

Pine nuts, a handful

Fresh mint for garnishing

Salt

Pepper

Instructions

- Combine the 2 sliced onions, one and a half tablespoons of olive oil, ½ ounce ground sumac, 1 teaspoon cinnamon, ¼ teaspoon allspice, ¼ teaspoon ground cloves, and a pinch of saffron in a large, microwavable glass mixing bowl.

- Microwave the mixture for two and a half minutes. Stir the mixture and microwave again for another two and a half minutes.

- Plop in the boneless chicken thighs into the slow cooker.

- Season with pepper and salt then add the onion mixture from the microwave oven. Stir enough to make sure the chicken thighs are nestling on the onion mixture.

- Cover and set the temperature on low. Cook for 6 hours.

Before serving, sauté a handful of pine nuts in a little olive oil until browned. Chop the fresh mint for use as garnishing together with the pine nuts.

#22 Crockpot Puerco Pibil

Ingredients

1 onion, medium

1 can fire-roasted tomato, diced (15 oz)

2 tbsp annato powder

1 tsp cumin powder

1 tsp black pepper, ground

1 tsp salt

Nutmeg, 1 pinch

5 lb pork shoulder roast

Juice of 1 orange

1/4 cup apple cider vinegar

2 tsp salt

Instructions

- Combine 2 tbsp of annatto powder, 1 teaspoon ground cumin, 1 teaspoon ground black pepper, 1 teaspoon salt and a pinch of nutmeg together in a small bowl. Stir in some water a little at a time until the spice mixture has a thickened like a paste.

- Slice the onion and sauté on a skillet over medium heat using a spoonful of coconut oil. Continue to sauté until the onion slices are translucent, and then add 1 can of fire-roasted tomatoes. Continue to cook until the tomatoes have softened.

- Trim the pork shoulder roast of any visible excess fat. Slice the fat-trimmed pork roast into long cuts about 1 ½ inches wide. Rub each slice with salt.

- Pour the juice of one orange into the crockpot together with 1/4 cup cider vinegar. Stir in the annatto-spice paste until fully dissolved. Lay down the pork slices into the liquid in the crockpot. Pour the sautéed tomato-onion mixture on top.

- Cover and set the temperature on low. Cook for 6 to 8 hours.

#23 Apple Pork Tenderloin

Ingredients

4 Organic Gala Apples

1.5 to 2 lb Pork Tenderloin

Nutmeg

2 Tbsp Raw Honey

Instructions

- Core and then slice 4 organic Gala apples.

- Layer the apple slices at the bottom of the slow cooker and sprinkle generously with nutmeg.

- Cut some slits in the pork tenderloin. If necessary you can halve the tenderloin so you can fit them nicely inside the slow cooker.

- Place one apple slice in each of the slits you made in the tenderloin.

- With the apple slices firmly in place in the slits, arrange the tenderloin pieces on top the layer of apple slices inside the slow cooker. Again, sprinkle the top generously with nutmeg.

- Place whatever remaining apple slices there are on top of the pork tenderloin and sprinkle with nutmeg once more.

- Cover and set the temperature on low. Cook for 6 to 8 hours.

#24 Cranapple Turkey Breast

Ingredients

One 5 to 6 lbs turkey breast, bone-in, skin-on

3 apples, peeled, sliced

4 cups raw cranberries

1/2 cup apple cider vinegar

Salt

½ cup maple syrup

Instructions

- Place turkey breast in a large slow cooker.
- Sprinkle the turkey breast with salt.
- Arrange the apple slices and raw cranberries around the turkey breasts.

- Pour ½ cup apple cider vinegar and ½ cup maple syrup over the top making sure the turkey breasts are all covered.

- Cover and set the temperature on low.

- Cook for 6 to 8 hours or until the turkey meat is completely cooked through and the apple slices and cranberries are softened.

- Once done, take out the turkey breast and place it on a serving dish big enough to accommodate it.

- Mash the cranberries and the apple slices a little and top the turkey breast with them.

- Serve hot.

#25 Greek Inspired Stuffed Chicken Breasts

Ingredients

4 to 6 chicken breasts, boneless

1 tbsp olive oil

½ diced onion

½ red pepper, sliced thinly into strips

2 pcs pepperoncini peppers, sliced thinly into strips

6 oz spinach, fresh

2 tsp garlic, minced

1 ½ tsp of fresh oregano

Salt   Pepper

A squeeze of lemon

A cup of chicken stock

½ cup of white wine

1/3 cup of feta cheese

Fresh parsley for topping

Instructions

- With a sharp knife, form a deep pocket on one side of each chicken breast by cutting a deep slit that runs in the middle of each breast.

- Rub both sides of the chicken breast liberally with salt and pepper then set aside.

- Pour 1 tbsp olive oil on a skillet placed over medium heat. Sauté the diced onions and pepper strips for 1 to 2 minutes.

- Stir in 2 tsp minced garlic and 6 ounces fresh spinach and continue to cook until the spinach has wilted.

- Add in 1 ½ tsp of fresh oregano plus another dash of pepper and salt before removing from the heat.

- Stuff each chicken breast pocket with one heaping teaspoon of feta making sure that the feta is stuffed deep in each pocket.

- Spoon in the same amounts of the sautéed spinach-pepper mixture into each pocket. Place the stuffed chicken breasts in a slow cooker and squeeze fresh lemon juice over them.

- Add one cup of chicken stock and ½ cup white wine.

- Cover and set the temperature on low. Cook for 6 to 8 hours (4 hours on high).

- Serve with any toppings you desire.

#26 Paleo Crockpot Jambalaya Soup

Ingredients

5 cups chicken stock.

Chop 4 peppers of different colors

1 chopped onion, large

1 can diced tomatoes, large, organic

2 cloves of garlic, diced

2 bay leafs

1 lb shrimp, large, de-veined, raw

4 oz. diced chicken

1 pack Andouille sausage, spicy

1 head cauliflower

2 cups okra

3 tbsp Cajun Seasoning

1/4 cup hot sauce

To Make Your Own Cajun Seasoning

2 1/2 tbsp paprika

2 tsp salt

2 tbsp garlic powder

1 tbsp cayenne pepper

1 tbsp onion powder

1 tbsp black pepper

1 tbsp dried oregano

1 tbsp dried thyme

Instructions

- Put 4 chopped different colored peppers, 1 large chopped onion, diced garlic (2 cloves), 4 ounces of diced chicken, 3 tbsp of your own Cajun seasoning, and 2 bay leaves in a slow cooker. Pour in 5 cups of chicken stock.

- Cover and set the temperature on low. Cook for 6 hours.

- 30 minutes before the time is up, plop in the cut up Andouille sausages.

- Make your cauliflower rice by pulsing 1 head of chopped up raw cauliflower in a food processor until it has the consistency of rice.

- Add in the raw shrimp and the cauliflower rice in the last 20 minutes of cooking.

- Enjoy.

#27 Easy Crockpot Lamb Roast

Ingredients

2 lb lamb roast

2 cans green chile, diced (8oz ea)

1 can of fired roasted tomatoes, diced (14.5 oz)

1 pack of frozen bell peppers diced

1 tbsp cumin

1 tbsp paprika

1 tsp chili powder

1 tsp garlic powder

Salt

Pepper

Instructions

- Place 2 pounds of lamb roast in a slow cooker.

- Pour in 2 cans of diced green chili, 1 can of fire-roasted tomatoes and 1 pack of frozen bell peppers (diced).

- Add all the listed spices to the slow cooker stirring well to make sure the spices are evenly incorporated with the vegetables.

- Cover and set the temperature on low. Cook for 7 hours.

- When the cooking is done shred the lamb roast using two forks before serving.

Makes 6 servings

Preparation Time: 10 minutes

Cooking Time: 7 hours

Total Processing Time: 7 hours, 10 minutes

#28 Crockpot Kimchi Chicken

Ingredients

1 cup chicken broth, low-sodium

4 scallions, sliced- separate green and white parts

Mince 6 cloves of garlic

1 tbsp coconut aminos

1 tbsp sesame oil, dark

Mince 1 tsp of fresh ginger

2 lbs chicken thighs, boneless, skinless

2 cups cabbage kimchi, drained

Instructions

- Combine all the listed ingredients in a slow cooker except for the 4 scallion greens, chicken thighs, and kimchi cabbage.

- Plop in the chicken thighs into the slow cooker making sure they are well nestled in the sauce. Spoon some of the sauce over the chicken thighs.

- Cover and set the temperature on low. Cook for 4 to 6 hours (closer to 4 hours is ideal).

- Before serving, set the temperature to high and add 2 cups of kimchi cabbage and cook for another 20 minutes.

- Sprinkle the top with scallion greens and serve.

#29 Crockpot Beef Tongue w/ Roasted Pepper Sauce

Ingredients

Tongue

1 beef tongue

1 sliced onion

3 cloves of garlic, crushed

3 bay leaves

Salt & pepper

Enough water to cover tongue in crockpot

Sauce

1 red pepper, peeled, diced and roasted

Dice 1 roasted serrano chili pepper

1 diced onion

Mince 3 cloves of garlic

20 oz tomatoes, sliced

6 oz tomato paste

1 tsp thyme

1 tsp oregano

Salt

Pepper

Instructions

Tongue

- Wash one beef tongue thoroughly with cold water. Dry by patting with paper towel.

- Line the bottom of your slow cooker with 1 sliced onion, 3 cloves of crushed garlic, and 3 bay leaves

- Lay the beef tongue on top of them and season generously with pepper and salt.

- Add enough water to completely submerge the beef tongue.

- Cover and set the temperature on low. Cook for 8 hours.

- When done, remove the beef tongue from slow cooker and peel off the outer skin of the tongue.

- Shred the shredded beef tongue and serve with the sauce below

To Make the Sauce

- Sauté 1 diced onion, minced garlic, diced roasted red pepper, and diced serrano chile in a saucepan over medium heat. Cook until the onions turn translucent.

- Add the rest of the sauce ingredients while stirring to blend well.

- Reduce to low heat and simmer for thirty minutes.

- Pour over the shredded tongue and serve.

Makes 4 servings

#30 Classic Corned Beef and Cabbage

Ingredients

6 carrots, organic, cut into chunks

Chop 2 organic onions

1 organic cabbage, wedged

2 to 3 lbs corned beef brisket w/ seasoning packet

2 to 3 cups water

Instructions

Preparation:

- Combine the carrot chunks, chopped onions, and cabbage wedges in a 4 to 6 quart slow cooker.

- Rinse the corned beef brisket under running cold water then pat dry using paper towels.

- Put the beef brisket into the slow cooker and sprinkle all the contents of the seasoning packet over it.

- Pour 2 to 3 cups of water over the beef brisket.

- Cover and set the temperature on low. Cook for 8 to 9 hours.

- When done, remove the corned beef brisket and wrap in aluminum foil. Place inside a 2000 F oven to keep it warm until serving time.

To serve:

- Cut the corned beef brisket into thin slices - cutting across grain.

- Remove the vegetables from the slow cooker using a slotted spoon. Place over the corned beef slices to serve.

Pour some of the cooking juices on top.

#31 Slow Cooked Buffalo Chicken Meatballs

Ingredients

1 lb. ground chicken

1/3 cup almond meal

1 egg 2 cloves garlic, minced

2 green onions, thinly sliced

3/4 cup buffalo sauce

Sea salt

Freshly ground black pepper

Instructions

- Preheat the oven to 4000 F.

- Combine one pound ground chicken with 1/3 cup of almond meal, 1 egg, minced garlic, sliced green onions in a bowl. Sprinkle with some pepper and salt.

- Mix everything into a well combined mass.

- Roll into 1 1/2-inch meatballs.

- Arrange the meatballs on a baking sheet and place inside the preheated oven. Bake the meatballs for 5 minutes.

- When done, remove the meatballs from the oven and plop in to your slow cooker.

- Add ¾ cup of buffalo sauce and stir.

Cover and set the temperature on low. Cook for 2 hours.

#32 Sweet &Savory Sage Stew w/ Pumpkin and Cherries

Ingredients

1 to 2 lbs stew meat, cubed

4 C of cubed butternut squash

1 onion, medium, chopped

1 C dried cherries

1 tbsp sage

1 tsp thyme

1 bay leaf

3 1/2 C beef stock

1 tsp allspice

1/2 tsp nutmeg

cup pumpkin puree

1 tbsp of butter

Salt

Instructions

- Place 1 tbsp of butter in a saucepan and put over medium heat to melt then sauté the chopped onions, 1 tbsp sage and 1 tsp thyme until the onions turn translucent.

- Sear quickly the stew meat cubes in a skillet over high heat until the meat cubes form brown crusts. There is no need to cook through the meat cubes.

- Add the seared meat cubes together with the onion mixture to the slow cooker. Add 3 ½ cups of beef stock, ½ tsp nutmeg, 1 bay leaf and 1 tsp allspice.

- Cover and set the temperature on low. Cook for at least 6 hours.

- When done, plop 4 cups of cubed butternut squash and 1 cup dried cherries. Cook for another 1 to 2 hours until the butternut squash has softened.

- Prior to serving stir in 1 cup of pumpkin puree. Adjust the taste by adding some pepper and salt.

#33 Crockpot Pepper Steak – Asian Version

Ingredients

1 can bean sprouts (16 oz), drained

2 tbsps of coconut oil

1/4 cups tamari

(Wheat-free)

2 lbs sirloin steak (any cut will do)

1 can of diced tomatoes (16 oz)

1 green pepper, large, sliced thinly

1 sliced onion, small

Mince 1 to 2 cloves of garlic

Salt

Pepper

Instructions

- Cut the sirloin steak at an angle on a chopping board to make strips around half an inch thick.

- Add 2 tbsp coconut oil in a frying pan (large) and heat. Once hot, sauté the sirloin steak until it is slightly browned.

- Drain the excess fat and coat meat generously with ground pepper and then plop in the meat into the slow cooker.

- Add the minced garlic and ¼ cup wheat-free tamari. Mix until the meat is completely coated.

- Cover and set the temperature on low. Cook for around 6 hours.

- An hour prior to serving, add in 1 can of bean sprouts, 1 can diced tomatoes, 1 green pepper (cut into strips) and 1 sliced onion.

Set the cooker on high and cook for one more hour.

- Best served piping hot.

#34 Pork Lettuce Wraps – Asian Twist

Ingredients

For the chunk of meat

2-3 lbs of pork shoulder   Salt and pepper

3-4 smashed whole garlic cloves

Dash of garlic powder

For the sauce

2 tbsps of Almond Butter

4 tbsps of Coconut Aminos

2 tsps of Sesame Oil

2 tbsp Vinegar

1 tbsp Honey

1 tbsp Sriracha

1/2 tsp of Black Pepper

1 tbsp minced ginger

Instructions

1.Put the prepared pork shoulder in a slow cooker.

2.Whisk together 4 tbsp coconut aminos, 2 tbsp almond butter, 1 tbsp honey, 2 tbsp vinegar, 2 tsp sesame oil, 1 tbsp siracha, 1/2 tsp of black pepper and 1 tbsp minced ginger in a bowl to make the sauce.

3.Pour the sauce over the meat inside the slow cooker.

4.Cover and set the temperature on low. Cook for about 4 to 6 hours.

5.When done, shred the meat using two forks.

6.Serve on top of lettuce. Garnish with your favorites before serving if you wish.

#35 Mexican Pulled Chicken Stuffed Peppers

Ingredients

4 bell peppers, large

3 to 4 chicken breasts

2 tbsp jalapenos, chopped

1 cup diced tomatoes

1/2 cup tomato juice canned

1/4 cup onion, finely minced

1/4 cup green peppers, chopped

2 cups salsa

shredded cheese

1 pack taco seasoning (or you can make your own) homemade taco seasoning recipe:

1 tsp salt

2 tsp. onion powder

1 tsp chili powder

1/2 tsp crushed red pepper,

1/2 tsp garlic powder

1/4 tsp oregano

½ to 1 tsp ground cumin

Instructions

- Plop in the whole chicken breasts together with all the listed ingredients in a slow cooker.

- Stir, cover, and set the temperature on low. Cook for 6 to 8 hours.

- When done, shred the chicken breasts using two forks. Mix the shredded chicken with the ingredients in the slow cooker.

- With a sharp knife, cut off the top of the 4 large bell peppers and scoop out the inside ribs and the seeds.

- Run the bell peppers under cold water to remove whatever remaining seeds are still inside.

- Stuff the bell peppers with the chicken mixture from the slow cooker. Pour some salsa (cooking juice from the cooker) so they won't dry out when baked.

- Arrange the stuffed bell peppers in a baking dish and place in a 3500 oven. Bake for 20 minutes until the bell peppers have softened. Top the stuffed bell peppers with shredded cheese and some salsa.

#36 Crockpot BOEUF BOURGUIGNON

Ingredients

4 slices bacon, cut into 1" pieces

2 lbs beef stew meat

1-2 large carrots, peeled and cut into chunks

1 cup frozen pearl onions

1/2 tsp marjoram leaves, dried

Mince 2 cloves of garlic

1/2 C red wine, dry

1/2 cup beef broth

1 tbsp Worcestershire sauce   Grind

1/2 oz of dried porcini mushrooms

8 oz crimini mushrooms sliced   Salt and pepper

Instructions

- Cook the bacon pieces in a skillet until crisp. Remove and set on paper towels to cool and drain.

- Remove some of the excess fat from the skillet but leave about one teaspoon for browning.

- Cut the beef stew meat into cubes and put into the skillet over high heat to sear until the outside has slightly browned.

- Remove the beef cubes and deglaze the skillet by pouring and mixing 1/4 cup of water. Add this skillet juice to the slow cooker together with browned beef cubes and the bacon pieces.

- Add the carrot chunks, pearl onion, and minced garlic.

- Combine ½ cup of red wine, ½ cup beef broth, 1 tbsp Worcestershire sauce, ½ ounce ground porcini mushroom, and ½ tsp ground marjoram leaves in a bowl. Mix well and pour the mixture over the ingredients in the slow cooker.

- Adjust the taste with some pepper and salt.

- Cover and set the temperature on low. Cook for 6 to 8 hours.

- Prior to serving, sauté the crimini mushrooms in a little olive oil until they are slightly browned. Combine the browned mushrooms with the beef mixture.

- Serve on top of mashed cauliflower.

#37 Crockpot Italian Meat Balls

Ingredients

1 lb ground beef

1 lb turkey sausage

1/2 cup finely chopped onion

1/4 cup almond flour

1 egg 1 tbsp Italian seasoning

1 tbsp basil

1 tbsp minced garlic,

1/2 tsp onion salt

28 oz. crushed tomatoes

Instructions

- Place all the listed ingredients except the crushed tomatoes in a large bowl and mix thoroughly.

- Hand-shape the mixture into meatballs the size of a golf ball.

- Brush the inside of a slow cooker lightly with some olive oil and plop in the meatballs.

- Pour the crushed tomatoes over meatballs.

- Cover and set the temperature on low. Cook for 6 hours (4 hours on high).

- Serve hot with a small salad on the side if you desire.

#38 Paleo Braised Beef Shanks

Ingredients

2 beef shanks, large (7-8oz each)

4 cloves of garlic, large, smashed

a splash of red wine

1 to 2 sprigs of fresh rosemary

Sea salt

black pepper, cracked

1 to 3 cups chicken stock (must cover ¾ of the meat)

1 tbsp of extra virgin coconut oil

2 to 3 cups raw kale,

roughly chopped

1/4 tsp onion powder

Instructions

- Plop in all the listed ingredients in a slow cooker.

- Cover and set the temperature on low. Cook for 4 to 6 hours until the meat is so tender that it falls apart when touched with a fork.

- When cooking is nearly done prepare the kale. Place 1 tbsp of coconut oil in a skillet over medium heat and place the chopped kale to cook until softened.

- Top the braised beef shanks with the chopped kale to serve.

#39 Salsa Pork Chops

Ingredients

4 pork sirloin chops, fat trimmed

1/2 tsp ground cumin

1/2 tsp garlic powder

1/2 tsp. Vege-Sal

1/2 tsp ground black pepper, fresh

1 tbsp olive oil

1 cup of salsa

2 tbsp of fresh-squeezed lime juice,

Note: Add 1

1/2 cups salsa and

3 tbsp limejuice if you want more sauce.

Instructions

- Trim the pork sirloin chops of all visible fat around the edges and discard the excess fat.

- Combine ½ tsp ground cumin, ½ tsp garlic powder, ½ tsp Vege-Sal or salt, and ½ tsp fresh ground black pepper in a small bowl to make a spice mixture.

- Rub both sides of the fat-trimmed pork sirloin chops thoroughly with the spice mixture.

- Heat 1 tbsp olive oil in a heavy frying pan over medium heat. Add the pork chops and cook for 5 minutes per side until nicely browned.

- Brush the sides and bottom of the slow cooker with a little olive oil then plop in the browned pork chops.

- Mix 1 cup of salsa with 2 tbsp of fresh squeezed limejuice. Pour the mixture over the pork chops.

- Cover and set the temperature on high. Cook for 2-3 hours until the pork chops are tender enough when pierced with a fork. Spoon some of the sauce and pour over the pork chops before serving.

#40 Lamb Ribs Curry w/ Sweet Onions and Fresh Garlic

Ingredients

2 lbs. lamb ribs, thawed   Mince

1 head of garlic

Chop 1 sweet onions

2 tbsp red curry paste or curry powder

3 tbsp organic butter

Instructions

- Heat 1 tsp of butter in a sauté pan and place the lamb ribs. Sear both sides of each rib.

- Plop the seared lamb ribs into the slow cooker.

- Combine all the other listed ingredients into a rubbing mixture and spread it liberally all over the lamb ribs.

Cover and set the temperature on low. Cook for 8 hours.

#41 Cambodian Lime Ginger & Honey Ribs

Ingredients

6 quart crockpot

2-3 lbs boneless country style pork ribs

1/4 C fresh ginger, grated

Crush 6 cloves of garlic

3 1/2 tbsp honey

3 tbsp coconut aminos

3 tbsp fish sauce

Grate 1 tbsp of black pepper

1 tbsp salt

1/4 C lime juice

for dipping sauce:

2 tbsp lime juice

2 tbsp coconut aminos

black pepper, freshly cracked   white pepper, freshly cracked

Instructions

- Sear the pork ribs in a sauté pan for a few minutes to brown. Pat them dry with paper towel before plopping them into the slow cooker.

- Combine all the remaining ingredients (except ingredients for dipping sauce) to make the marinade mixture.

- Pour the marinade mixture on top of the pork ribs.

- Cover and set the temperature on low. Cook for 8 hours.

- For the dipping sauce just mix all the dipping sauce ingredients listed above.

- Serve alongside the pork ribs.

#42 Paleo Crockpot Fudge

Ingredients

2 qt crockpot

coconut oil

2 1/2 C chocolate chips (dairy, soy, and nut free!)

1/2 C coconut milk

1/4 C honey

1/8 tsp sea salt

1 tsp vanilla extract

Instructions

•Grease the inside surfaces of a slow cooker liberally with coconut oil.

•Empty a can of coconut milk into a bowl and stir until it has a uniform consistency.

•Transfer half a cup of the coconut milk into the slow cooker.

•Add the remaining listed ingredients except the vanilla extract.

•Cover and set the temperature on high. Cook for 2 hours.

- Add 1 tsp vanilla extract and stir well then turn off the slow cooker.

- Leave the slow cooker uncovered for 3 to 4 hours until it is at room temperature.

- After cooling down to room temperature, spoon-stir the mixture continuously for about 10 minutes until its glossy finish is all gone.

- Grease a 1-quart container with coconut oil, and pour the fudge mixture to it.

- Refrigerate the fudge mixture overnight.

- Cut it into bite sizes and serve.

#43Paleo Crab Chili Chowder

Ingredients

6 quart crock pot

2 tbsp butter

1 chopped onion

4 cups chicken broth

1 chopped potato

1/3 tsp thyme

1 can green chile,

(4 oz), drained

1 sups sweet corn kernels

1 can crabmeat,

12 oz

1/2 tsp chili paste

salt

pepper

1 cup heavy cream avocado slices (for garnishing)

Instructions

•Heat 2 tbsp butter on a skillet over a stove top. Sauté 1 chopped onion until they turn translucent.

Scrape the sautéed onions together with the butter into a slow cooker.

- Add the rest of the listed ingredients to the slow cooker except the heavy cream and avocado slices.

 They will be added later.

- Cover and set the temperature on low. Cook for 8 hours.

- Once the cooking is done, you may serve it as it is or you can puree it further using a hand blender until

 it has a chowder-like smooth consistency.

- Spoon the mixture while hot into soup bowls. Top with fresh avocado slices before serving.

#44 Paleo Orange Chicken

Ingredients

6 quart crock pot

2 lbs of skinless & deboned chicken thighs

5 tsp tomato paste

1/8 C orange juice

4 tbsp coconut aminos

3 tbsp honey

1 tsp sesame oil

Mince 2 cloves of garlic

1/2" pc fresh ginger, grated

1/2 tsp rice vinegar

1/2 tsp red chili paste

2 tbsp arrowroot powder

salt

pepper

Instructions

- Plop 2 lbs of boneless and skinless chicken thighs into the bottom of a slow cooker.

- Combine the remaining listed ingredients except for the arrowroot powder in a large bowl. Slather the mixture over the chicken thighs.

- Cover and set the temperature on low. Cook for 7-8 hours (4 hours on high). Be sure the chicken is thoroughly cooked before removing it from the slow cooker.

- Remove and set aside the chicken thighs.

- Add 2 tbsp of arrowroot powder to the cooking juice left in the slow cooker and mix well.

- Cover the slow cooker and set the temperature on high. Cook for 15 more minutes until the liquid has thickened.

- Serve the chicken thighs over cauliflower rice or steamed broccoli and carrots. Ladle some of the orange sauce from the slow cooker and pour over the top of the chicken thighs.

#45 Crockpot Stuffed Cabbage Rolls

Ingredients

For the rolls:

12 leaves of cabbage

1 cup rice, cooked

1 egg, beaten

1 clove garlic, finely chopped

1/4 cup of milk

1 lb of lean ground turkey

1/4 cup white onion, finely chopped

For the sauce:

1 1/4 tsp salt

1 1/4 tsp ground black pepper

1 tsp Worcestershire sauce

1 can (15 oz) tomato sauce,

2 tbsp catsup

1/2 tsp dried thyme leaves

2 tbsp lemon juice

1 tsp paprika

2 tbsp honey

1 tsp salt

Instructions

- Bring a pot of salted water and bring to a boil over high heat. Once boiling, drop the cabbage leaves and let it boil for 2 more minutes.

- Combine 1 can of tomato sauce, 1 tsp of Worcestershire sauce, all the listed spices, 2 tbsp catsup, 2 tbsp lemon juice, 1 ¼ tsp black pepper, 1 tsp salt and 2 tbsp of raw honey in a small bowl. Whisk and blend into a sauce.

- In a separate bowl, combine 1 lb of lean ground turkey together with 1 cup cooked rice, 1 beaten egg, chopped garlic, ¼ cup finely chopped white onion, and ¼ cup milk.

- Stir in 1/4 of the tomato sauce mixture and whisk.

- Scoop about 1/4 cup of the turkey mixture into the mid section of each cabbage leaf. Roll up each cabbage leaf at the same time tucking in the ends tightly.

- Arrange the cabbage rolls at the bottom of a slow cooker. Top with the remaining tomato sauce mixture.

- Cover the cooker and set the temperature on low. Cook for 8 to 9 hours (4 to 5 hours on high).

#46 Dijon Brussel Sprouts with Bacon Ends

Ingredients

1 lb Brussel sprouts		1 tbsp Dijon

A dash of salt		A dash of pepper

2 tbsp butter		5 to 6 oz bacon ends, crisply cooked

Instructions

- Cut the bacon ends into bite-sized pieces.

- Wash and trim the ends the Brussels sprouts.

- Cut each brussel sprout in half and plop into a slow cooker along with the bite-sized bacon ends.

- Add the rest of the listed ingredients into the slow cooker.

- Cover and set the temperature on low. Cook for 4 to 5 hours.

#47 Acorn Squash Stuffed with Cinnamon, Apple, and Turkey

Ingredients

1 acorn squash, medium 1 pound ground turkey

1 teaspoon cinnamon powder   1/2 apple, chopped into small bite sized pieces

1/4 cup of pecan nuts   1 teaspoon nutmeg powder

1 cup raisins 1/2 chopped onion

A dash of cloves

Instructions

- Brown 1 lb of ground turkey in a large skillet stir cooking continuously. Toss in the bite-sized apple pieces, ½ chopped onions, a dash of cloves, 1 tsp nutmeg, and 1 tsp cinnamon once the ground turkey is slightly brown.

- Stir-cook for 6 to 8 minutes over low heat until the apple pieces are softened and the onions turn translucent.

- Remove the pan from heat then add ¼ cup pecan nuts and 1 cup of raisins. Set aside for a while.

- Slice the acorn squash in half and remove the seeds. Place the acorn squash halves at the bottom of the slow cooker.

- Spoon the turkey mixture into each of the squash halves. Do not let any of the turkey mixture fall into the bottom of the cooker.

- Once the squash halves have been filled with the turkey mixture, pour one cup of water into the bottom of the slow cooker.

- Cover and set the temperature on low. Cook for 4 hours.

- To check if the squash is already tender, pierce it with a fork. Cook longer if necessary.

#48 COFFEE BRAISED BEEF CHILE

Ingredients

1 beef roast round Mince 4 cloves of garlic

2 teaspoons cocoa powder   3 tablespoon of ancho chile powder

1 teaspoon oregano   1/2 teaspoon chipotle powder (if you want it hot)

1 teaspoon cumin powder   1/8 teaspoon cinnamon

1/2 tsp salt, or to taste   3/4 cup brewed coffee, strong preferably cold brewed

1 tablespoon balsamic vinegar 1/2 red onion, large, sliced

Instructions

- Combine all spices (3 tbsp ancho chile, 1 tsp oregano, 1/8 tsp cinnamon. 1 tsp Cumin, ½ tsp chipotle) with 2 tsp cocoa powder in a small bowl. Add a little water to form into a loose paste.

- Rub the beef roast rounds with your newly prepared spice paste making sure all sides are well coated.

•Spread out the onion slices at the bottom of the slow cooker. Lay the spiced beef roast round on top of the onion slices.

•Mix 1 tbsp of balsamic vinegar with 3/4 cup brewed coffee and pour the mixture all over the beef roast evenly.

•Cover and set the temperature on low. Cook for 6 to 8 hours.

#49 Crockpot Chicken Stroganoff

Ingredients

1-1 1/2 lbs chicken breast, boneless, skinless, cut into cubes Slice 8 ounces of mushrooms

1/2 cup of white cooking wine   2 tbsp butter

1 package salad dressing mix (.7-oz), dry Italian-style 6 to 8 ounces cream cheese (reduced-fat)

1 can cream-of-chicken soup (10.75-oz), reduced-fat, low sodium

Instructions

• Put all the listed ingredients (except cream of chicken soup and the cream cheese) in the crockpot.

• Mix a little to make sure the ingredients are well combined.

• Cover and set the temperature on low. Cook for 5 to 6 hours.

• When the time is up, stir in 6 to 8 ounces of cream cheese and 1 can cream of chicken soup.

• Cover the cooker once more and set the temperature on high. Cook for another 30 minutes.

#50 Slow Cooker Chicken Cacciatore

Ingredients

1 chopped medium onion   1 chopped red bell pepper,

1 cup diced of mushrooms   3 to 4 lbs of skinless deboned chicken breasts

2 minced garlic cloves   1 can diced tomatoes (14.5 ounces)

3 tbsp tomato paste   1 cup of gluten free chicken broth

½ cup white wine   ⅛ tsp pepper

½ tsp salt   1 tsp Italian seasoning

3 tbsp corn starch   1 bay leaf

3 tbsp water

Instructions

- Place the minced garlic, ½ tsp pepper, and chopped onion at the bottom of the slow cooker.

- Arrange the boneless, skinless chicken breasts on top.

- Empty 1 can of diced tomatoes along with its juice into a bowl. Add 3 tbsp tomato paste, 1 cup of gluten-free chicken broth, ½ cup white cooking wine, ½ tsp pepper, ½ tsp salt, 1 tsp Italian seasoning, and 1 bay leaf. Mix and pour over the chicken breasts.

- Cover and set the temperature on low. Cook for 7 to 8 hours (3 to 4 hours on high).

- Once the time is up, remove the chicken breast and set aside for a while.

- Mix 3 tbsp of corn starch with 3 tbsp of water and combine the mixture with the cooking juice in the slow cooker.

- Cover and set on high. Cook for 30 minutes until the mixture is thick enough for you.

- Pour the sauce from the slow cooker over the chicken thighs and serve.

Chapter 6 - Frequently Asked Questions about Slow Cookers

Before you start rolling up your sleeves and start your slow cooking journey, let's us try to iron out some possible kinks that may still be lurking in your minds. Here are some of the most frequently asked questions about slow cooking.

1. *Do you have to stir the ingredients while cooking the dish?*

   There is no need to stir the ingredients. Don't forget that every time the slow cooker cover is opened you lose valuable heat, which requires longer cooking time.

2. *Can you really leave the slow cookers unattended?*

   Yes. The main feature of a slow cooker is you can 'set and forget' it. You can simply plop in your ingredients, set the temperature and timer and leave. The low temperature setting has an approximate temperature of only 200^0 F, so there is no problem of overcooking or scorching. The slow cooker also operates on a very low wattage (120 watts), which means the electrical consumption won't be that much.

3. *How big a slow cooker should I use?*

   The size of the slow cooker to use will depend on how many people you will be preparing the meal for. If it is only for a small family or for a couple, a 3 to 3 ½ quarts slow cooker will do. If you are feeding a large family, you may need a 5 to 6 quart capacity slow cooker. If you are doing a batch cooking session with the intention of cooking more to serve a portion and freeze the rest for a later date, then you may need a 5 to 6 quart size slow cooker.

4. *How do I thicken the juice when it ends up being watery at the end of cooking time?*

    You can do two things to thicken the juice. One is to take off the cover and set the temperature to high. Allow it to cook uncovered for 20 to 30 minutes or until most of the juice has evaporated and the remaining juice is thick enough for you. The second is to stir in 1 to 2 tablespoons of almond flour, set the temperature to high, and cook for 10 minutes or until the juice is thick enough.

5. Can you prepare whole chickens, meat roasts, and other meats in a slow cooker to the correct doneness so that they can be perfectly sliced with ease?

    Of course you can. The best way is to use a meat thermometer and cook the meat at the recommended temperature for the particular type of meat you are cooking.

    You may also consider lining the sides and bottom of the pot with two to three times thickness of aluminum foil before putting in the roast. This will allow you to remove the whole chicken or the meat roast with great ease.

6. *Can I use the slow cooker to cook meals faster?*

    If you wish to cook meals faster, all you need to do is set the temperature to high and adjust the cooking time according to the chart below. Normally, slow cooker recipes use the low temperature setting over a longer period. This should not be problem if you follow the conversion table below for the cooking times.

Low	High
7 hours	3 hours
8 hours	4 hours
9 hours	5 hours
10 hours	6 hours

11 hours	7 hours
12 hours	8 hours

You need to consult your slow cooker manual though because different manufacturers have different recommended conversion times.

Some more tips to get you ready for slow cooking:

- There is no particular order to follow when putting the ingredients into the slow cooker. If there is, the recipe will clearly state so. If the size of the slow cooker is not stated in the recipe you can safely assume that it is a 3 1.2 to 4 quart capacity slow cooker. Otherwise, the recipe will clearly state the specific size of the slow cooker to use.

- Never make the mistake of filling the slow cooker to the brim. You have to give whatever you are cooking some space to simmer. You should leave at least 2 inches of free space between the top of the ingredient-filled crockpot and the lid.

- The slow cooker must be at least half full to cook properly if you are cooking stews and soup. Otherwise, you need to cut down on the cooking time. If the slow cooker is less than half full, you have to check the doneness every now and then to prevent over cooking.

- If you are cooking breads or cakes in the slow cooker, never open the cover or the lid within the 1½ to 2 hours of cooking time.

Conclusion

Thank you again for downloading this book!

I hope this book was able to help you get started on your Paleo slow-cooking journey and cooking your way to great health.

The next step is to use everything you learned from this book and start preparing your own Paleo and gluten-free meals. As you must have noticed from the recipes, it is not really that hard to stick to a Paleo lifestyle. All it takes is a lot of patience and determination and a little passion for making home-cooked meals. Remember, it is better to spend time and effort preparing healthy meals today, than pay for the medical bills later when life starts billing your family for your neglect.

Part 2

Crockpot Pulled Pork Chili

- Prep Time :10 Mins
- Cook Time : 10 Hours
- Total Time : 10 Hours 10 Mins
- Serves: 6-8

Ingredients

- 2 Pound Pork Roast
- 3 Garlic Cloves, Peeled
- ½ Cup Hot Sauce
- 3 Tablespoons Smoked Paprika
- 2 Tablespoons Garlic Powder
- 2 Tablespoon Chili Powder
- 1 Tablespoon Cumin
- 2 Teaspoons Cayenne Pepper
- 1 Heaping Tablespoon Red Pepper Flakes
- Lots Of Salt
- 2 Yellow Onions, Diced
- 1 Red Bell Pepper, Diced
- 1 Yellow Bell Pepper, Diced
- 2 (14) Ounce Cans Of Fire Roasted Tomatoes
- 1 (14) Ounce Can Of Tomato Sauce

- Avocado, Sliced (To Garnish)
- Green Onions, Diced (To Garnish)

How to make it:

1. Take a crock pot or slow cooking pot and put the roasted pork in it.
2. Make some holes in the pork roast with a sharp tool like a knife and add cloves of garlic after peeling the skin of the garlic.
3. To spice it up, put garlic powder, cumin, cayenne, paprika & some pepper flakes.
4. Before that, do not forget to add the hot or spicy sauce on it.
5. Now lay over the tomatoes, minced onions, pepper and tomato sauce over the pork. Use perfectly cut slices of green onions & avocado to embellish the dish.
6. And before embellishing it, you have to cook it for eight to ten hours by setting the heat to low.

****

Slow Cooker Paleo BBQ Brisket Recipe

- Prep Time : 5 Mins
- Total Time : 10 Hours 5 Mins
- Serves: 6 Servings :

Ingredients

- 3 Lb Brisket
- 10-12 Oz (300g) Tomato Paste
- 1 Cup (250ml) Water
- 1 Tablespoon Salt
- 2 Tablespoons Tamari Sauce (Or Coconut Aminos)
- 3 Tablespoons Raw Honey
- 2 Tablespoons Apple Cider Vinegar
- ½ Tablespoon Cinnamon Powder

How to make it

1. Take the constituents in a crock pot and blend them together.
2. Put the brisket in the crockpot and pour the sauce over it.

3. Heat it for ten to twelve hours at a low temperature.

4. Before eating, you should first bring out the brisket from the crockpot with some BBQ sauce.

5. And put the shredded brisket and sauce on the stove for a few minutes, less than five minutes would be proper.

6. The heat will lessen the sauce and a pinch of salt to make it better.

****

Paleo Slow Cooker Oxtail Stew Recipe

- Prep Time: 5 Mins
- Cook Time : 10 Hours 15 Mins
- Total Time : 10 Hours 20 Mins
- Serves: 4 Servings

Ingredients

- 4 Lb Oxtail (Chopped Into Segments - Get Your Butcher To Do This If Possible)

- 1-2 Cups Of Water (To Fill Up Half The Crockpot/Slowcooker)

- 2 14oz (400g) Cans Of Diced Tomatoes (Or 10 Fresh Tomatoes, Diced)

- 10 Cloves Garlic, Crushed

- 4 Teaspoons Paprika (Add More If Preferred)

- 2 Tablespoons Italian Seasoning (Optional - Great Instead Of Paprika E.G., F You Don't Like Any Heat In Your Stew)

- Dash Of Chili Powder (Optional)

- Salt To Taste

How to make it

1. At first you should take a crockpot, and put some water in it.

2. Put the oxtail into the water and heat it for around ten hours. The setting for the heat should be low.

3. When the meat is soft and tender, it's ready to be added to the stew.

4. The stew could be made in a stewpot or saucepan where tomatoes, spices and garlic is combined with the oxtail.

5. Cook it for under quarter of an hour, and your oxtail stew is ready to be served.

6. Do not forget to put some salt in it.

. ************

Homemade Thai Chicken Broth

- Prep Time : 5 Mins
- Total Time : 8 Hours 5 Mins
- Serves: 10+ Servings

Ingredients

- 1 Whole Chicken
- 1 Stalk Of Lemongrass, Cut Into Large Chunks
- 20 Fresh Basil Leaves (10 For The Slow Cooker, And 10 For Garnish)
- 5 Thick Slices Of Fresh Ginger
- 1 Lime
- 1 Tablespoon Salt
- Additional Salt To Taste

How to make it

1. Begin with a slow cooker or crockpot and put lemongrass, ten basil leaves, salt, ginger and the before all that put the chicken in the crock pot.
2. Put water in the crock pot and heat it for less than 10 hours.
3. Take a small bowl and use a ladle or dipper and put the blended broth into the bowl and decorate it with basil leaves.

4. And also put some salt and limejuice to make it taste better.

5. And your Thai chicken broth is ready to be consumed.

******

Slow Cooker Paleo Jerk Chicken

- Prep Time 10 Mins
- Total Time5 Hours 10 Mins
- Serves: 4 Servings

Ingredients

- 5 Drumsticks And 5 Wings (Or You Can Use A Whole Chicken Or 5 Chicken Breasts)
- 4 Teaspoons Of Salt

- 4 Teaspoons Of Paprika
- 1 Teaspoons Of Cayenne Pepper
- 2 Teaspoons Of Onion Powder
- 2 Teaspoons Of Thyme
- 2 Teaspoons Of White Pepper
- 2 Teaspoons Of Garlic Powder
- 1 Teaspoons Of Black Pepper

How to make it:-

1. Take all the spices and blend it in a container.
2. To make it non-spicy, just put onion powder in the place of cayenne pepper.
3. Use clean water to cleanse the chicken properly and apply the blend on to the chicken in the container.
4. The chicken would be little bit hot or spicy because of the paprika present in the spices.

5. Putting the blend inside the skin of the chicken would make it better.
6. For this purpose chicken drumsticks and wings are better .
7. As it is easier to place the blend in the wings and the drumstick.
8. Now put the chicken pieces inside the crock pot. Cook it for five or six hours and the heat should be fixed at 325 Degrees Fahrenheit, or at medium or low setting.
9. The meat is done when it gets separated. When that happens, your Paleo Jerk Chicken is ready to be served; you can serve it with bone or without it.

******

Slow Cooker Bacon & Chicken

- Serves: 4 Servings

Ingredients

- 5 Chicken Breasts
- 10 Slices Of Bacon
- 2 Tablespoons Thyme (Dried)
- 1 Tablespoon Oregano (Dried)
- 1 Tablespoon Rosemary (Dried)
- 5 Tablespoons Olive Oil (2 Tablespoons For The Slow Cooker And 3 Tablespoons After Cooking)
- 1 Tablespoon Salt

How to make it

1. First take a crock pot and blend all the items.
2. The heat should be set to low. Heat it for around eight hours.
3. When it's done, you need to put around three tablespoons of olive oil in the meat but before that the meat has to be cut into pieces or has to be shredded perfectly.

4. Your slow cooker bacon is ready to be enjoyed!

******

Paleo Ropa Vieja Recipe

- Prep Time20 Mins
- Total Time20 Mins
- Serves: 6-8 Servings

Ingredients

- 3lb Flank Steak
- 2 Tablespoons Coconut Oil (For Pan Searing)
- ¼ Cup Olive Oil
- 1 Tablespoon White Wine Vinegar
- 2 Tablespoons Of Sea Salt

- ¼ Cup Cilantro, Finely Chopped
- ¼ Cup Parsley, Finely Chopped
- 2 Cloves Garlic, Crushed
- 2 (6oz) Cans Tomato Paste
- 3 Peppers, Sliced
- 1 Tablespoon Onion Flakes (Or Onion Powder)
- 1 Tablespoon Garlic Powder
- 1 Tablespoon Oregano
- 1 Tablespoon Cumin Powder

How to make it:-

1. First take the flank steak or a flat cut steak and use a sharp tool to divide into two inch thick pieces.
2. Then take a big fillet or greased up frying pan and put a tablespoon of coconut oil in it and turn the heat unto high.
3. Take the cut steak pieces (take only half at first) and sear it in the pan for around two-two three minutes, when one side is over, heat the other side.

4. And after it is finished, do the same thing with the rest of the pieces.

5. Now take all the items in a crockpot with the seared meat. Blend it well, if need be combine everything with your hands.

6. Now heat up the crockpot, set it to low and continue heating it for six hours or so with the mix.

7. After it's over the meat has to be shredded or cut up into small fragments and blend everything well.

8. It's now ready to be served and enjoyed!

******

Slow Cooked Corned Beef Brisket and Roasted Cabbage

Ingredients:-

Slow Cooked Corned Beef Brisket

- 2½ Lb Corned Beef Brisket

- ½ Medium Onion
- 1 Carrot
- 1 Celery Stalk
- 1 Cup Chicken Or Beef Stock

Roasted Cabbage

- 1 Head Of Green Cabbage
- 1 Tablespoon Avocado Oil
- Salt And Pepper To Taste

How to make it

Slow Cooked Corned Beef Brisket

1. Take a slow cooker or crockpot and take diced onions, celery and carrot and put it on the base of the cooker.

2. Then put the corned beef on the vegetables and before that add the chicken stock or beef stock over the vegetables-celery, carrot and onions.

3. Heat the cooker for eight hours or less, the minimum time should be six hours.

4. And while heating it remember to put a lid over the cooker.

Roasted Cabbage

1. Set the oven temperature at 450 Degrees Fahrenheit.

2. Take a baking sheet and over it the cabbage which has been cut into eight pieces.

3. Use avocado oil, pepper and some salt over the sides.

4. Then take the pieces of cabbage in the oven for less than half an hour and continue to move it till the sides become brown and crunchy.

5. When it has reached this stage your cabbage roast is done and it is ready to be eaten.

Slow Cooker Lemongrass Coconut Chicken Drumsticks

Ingredients:-

- 10 Drumsticks, Skin Removed
- 1 Thick Stalk Fresh Lemongrass, Papery Outer Skins And Rough Bottom Removed, Trimmed To The Bottom 5 Inches
- 4 Cloves Garlic, Minced
- 1 Thumb-Size Piece Of Ginger, Microplaned
- 1 Cup Coconut Milk
- 2 Tablespoons red Boat Fish Sauce
- 3 Tablespoons Coconut Aminos
- 1 Teaspoon Five Spice Powder

- 1 Large Onion, Thinly Sliced
- ¼ Cup Fresh Cilantro, Chopped
- Kosher Salt
- Freshly Ground Pepper

How to make it

1. Take a pot or bowl where you have to make a soft and saucy blend with a blender.
2. And the blend or sauce would be made from lemongrass, ginger, garlic, coconut milk, fish sauce, coconut and mixed spices.
3. Now take another container where you have to put all the drumsticks and combine it with pepper and salt.
4. And blend it well with the marinade.
5. Put diced onions at the base of the crockpot and top it with the marinade and drumsticks.

6. The temperature should be set to low and heat it for around four to five hours.

7. Sprinkle some fish sauce, some black pepper and also add a little bit of salt over it after it has been cooked.

8. Finally, embellish it with some scallions or cilantro.

Slow Cooker Beef Stew with Cranberries and Rosemary

Ingredients:-

- 2 lbs. beef stew meat (cut into same size pieces)
- 2 bunches of radishes (scrubbed and trimmed, but left whole)
- 1 lb. celery root (peeled & cut into 1 inch cubes)
- 1 lb. carrots (peeled and thickly sliced)
- 3 cups bone broth

- 1 teaspoon salt (less if your broth is salted)
- 1/2 tsp. black pepper (optional – omit for AIP)
- 2 large onions (peeled whole)
- 2 large cloves garlic (peeled whole)
- 2 branches fresh rosemary
- 8 oz. bag of frozen cranberries (save these for the final step in the recipe)

How to make it

1. Start with a crockpot and put beef, radishes, carrots, celery root, bone broth, salt and pepper.
2. Combine it properly.
3. Put two onions, and then put two cloves of garlic over the onions.
4. At last put the rosemary branches over everything and cook it for around eight hours while setting the temperature to low.
5. When it is done, take the onions and garlic cloves out and put in a mixer blender, and use a dipper or

ladle to take out some broth, puree over the onions and the garlic.

6. After it has been blended, shift everything to the slow cooker and put frozen cranberries and mix it well.

7. Then put the lid and heat for another half an hour, while setting the temperature to low.

8. Salt can be adjusted according to taste.

9. Your stew is ready to be savored!

Slow Cooker Beef Stroganoff

Ingredients:-

- 2 lbs. beef stew meat
- 2 tsp. salt
- 1/2 tsp. pepper
- 1 tsp. garlic powder
- 2 tsp. paprika

- 1 tsp. thyme
- 1 tsp. onion powder
- 8 oz. sliced mushrooms
- 1/2 onion, sliced
- 1/3 c. coconut cream (scooped from the top of a refrigerated can of coconut milk)
- 2 tsp. red wine vinegar

How to make it

1. Begin with a small pot or bowl where you have to combine all the spices.
2. Then atke another large bowl or pot where the meat has to be kept.
3. Drizzle the meat with the spies. Blend everything properly with your hand.
4. Then put the thinly cut mushrooms and onions in a bowl in crockpot.
5. Then put the prepared beef in the crockpot.

6. Then you have to heat it for four and half hours. Remember to close the lid.

7. If the meat becomes soft then it is ready to be taken out.

8. Then put the coconut cream, vinegar, salt or pepper in the crockpot and blend it properly with a spoon.

9. Heat it without the cover for nearly an hour or so. Your dish is now ready to be served!

Crockpot Thai Beef Stew

- SERVES: 6-8
- PREP TIME:20mins
- COOK TIME:300-480 mins
- TOTAL TIME: 320 mins

Ingredients:-

- 2 tablespoons coconut oil, divided
- 3 pounds beef stew meat, trimmed of fat
- 1 medium yellow onion, thinly sliced

- 2 cloves garlic, minced
- 2 teaspoons peeled and minced fresh ginger
- 1 (13.5-ounce) can full-fat coconut milk
- 1/3 cup tomato paste
- 1/2 cup Thai red curry paste
- 2 tablespoons fish sauce
- 2 teaspoons fresh lime juice
- 2 teaspoons sea salt
- 2 cups broccoli florets
- 2 cups julienned carrots
- 1 cup peeled and julienned jicama*
- fresh cilantro, for garnish

How to make it:-

1. First take a skillet or frying pan and heat one tablespoon of coconut oil in it.
2. Set the temperature to medium high and put the meat, but not altogether.

3. Then take a slotted spoon for transferring batch of browned meat on the skillet.

4. Clean the bottom of the skillet for even cooking.

5. When it is done, clean the skillet and put one tablespoon of coconut oil, and fry onion, garlic, and ginger over medium heat for around five minutes.

6. Then put the coconut milk and blend it constantly, so that the excess small brown pieces or bits, reach the bottom.

7. Then pour the paste of tomato, curry, fish sauce lime juice and salt and put the mix on the beef, in the crockpot.

8. Heat it for five hours when the temperature is set to high and for eight hours when it's set to low. Embellish it with cilantro while serving it.

****

Slow Cooker Squeaky Clean Boeuf Bourgignon

- Yield: Serves 4 to 6

Ingredients:-

- 900g (2lbs) grass-fed beef stew meat
- 1 large onion, chopped
- 2 cloves garlic, chopped
- 2 large carrots, peeled and sliced
- 1 small (1½ cups) turnip, peeled and diced
- 2-3 sprigs fresh rosemary, whole
- 2 Bay leaves
- 1 tsp Himalayan salt
- 1 tsp freshly cracked black pepper
- 2 tbsp Dijon mustard
- 2 cups bone broth

- 1/4 cup red wine vinegar
- 227g (1/2lb) mushrooms, sliced
- 2 tbsp tapioca starch
- 2 tbsp water

How To Make It:-

1. The meat has to be dried first and put pepper and salt over it, liberally.
2. Take a skillet or a frying pan to melt ghee, lard or to fry coconut oil.
3. Set the temperature to high.
4. Then put the meat over the pan and there should be some space between the pieces.
5. Heat it till the point it changes its color to brown.
6. Take the meat pieces out in a bowl or pot so that the juices get drained.
7. And in the pan put some more oil if needed and fry the onion and garlic.

8. Blend it constantly. Put the broth, red wine vinegar, Dijon mustard and heat it.

9. Then again transfer the meat and juices over the skillet.

10. Then take all the things and shift it to a crockpot and put carrots, turnip, mushrooms, rosemary and bay leaves.

11. Heat it for eight hours by setting the temperature to low and for six hours by setting the temperature to high.

12. When it is cooked fully use a dipper to put it on a pot or saucepan, and boil it. And in another container, combine tapioca and water and then put it in the liquid.

13. Then take the sauce onto the crockpot and blend it till it gets smooth.

14. Top it with bay leaves and rosemary sprigs before serving it.

Slow-Cooker Beef Brisket With Bourbon BBQ Sauce

Ingredients

- 1 Batch Bourbon Spiked BBQ Sauce
- 1 3 To 4 Lb Beef Brisket
- 1 Onion, Sliced
- Salt, Pepper, Granulated Garlic
- 1 Tbs Coconut Oil, To Sear The Brisket

How to make it:-

1. At first prepare a Bourbon spiked BBQ sauce.
2. Then take a big skillet or deep frying pan, and heat some coconut oil in it.
3. Then put some salt, pepper, granulated garlic over the brisket.
4. Fry the brisket for 2 mins, flip the sides, till the meat has a good brown crust.
5. After that put some onions in the crockpot and put the fried brisket over that.

6. Then put the BBQ sauce over them. Blend them properly.
7. Then cover the slow cooker and heat for six to eight hours when the temperature is set to low.
8. When it is finished, the meat would be quite soft.
9. Before serving it, the beef has to be shredded into pieces, with a knife or a fork.

Roast Stew Paleo

- Prep time: 10 mins
- Cook time: 7 hours
- Total time: 7 hours 10 mins

Ingredients

- ½ pound of organic uncured bacon, in strips
- 2 to 3 pound grass-fed and -finished chuck roast

- 2 large organic red onions, peeled and cut in slices
- 1 clove organic garlic, peeled and smashed
- 1 small organic green or Savoy cabbage
- Celtic sea salt
- Fresh ground black pepper to taste
- 1 sprig fresh organic thyme
- 1 cup of homemade beef bone broth

How to make it:-

1. Start with a crockpot and put bacon pieces or slices in the crockpot.
2. Put some onion pieces and garlic; add the chuck roast, cabbage pieces, broth, thyme and some sea salt with generous amount of ground black pepper.
3. Heat the crockpot fro seven hours and set the temperature to low.
4. Now you can enjoy your stew in small bowls.

Slow Cooker Paleo Meatballs

Ingredients:-

- 3lbs Ground Beef
- 1/4 cup finely cut spinach
- 2 tbls finely chopped onion
- 1 tsp garlic salt
- salt and pepper
- oil
- favorite pasta sauce

How to make it:-

1. At first start with a mixing bowl or container and mix the spinach, onions, salt, garlic salt, salt and pepper with ground beef.

2. Blend it well. Then make a few meatballs, one or two inches in size.

3. Put them aside.
4. And take a skillet or frying pan and heat some oil in it.
5. Put the meatballs in the skillet and make it brown. Then put it in the crockpot and put some sauce over it.
6. Heat it for a four to five hours while setting the temperature to low.

Paleo Crockpot Shredded Beef

- Prep time: 5 mins
- Total time: 5 hours 5 mins

Ingredients:-

- 3.5 lb chuck / pot roast
- ¼ cup preferred stock
- ½ tsp salt

- 1 tsp black pepper
- ½ tblsp oregano
- ½ tsp cumin
- ¼ tsp ancho chile
- ¼ tsp paprika
- ⅛ tsp cinnamon
- ½ tsp garlic
- 2 tblsp tomato paste

For the sauce:

- ¾ cup skimmed stock / meat juices (see below)
- ¼ onion, diced
- 2 cloves garlic
- 1 jalapeno, diced
- ¼ tsp salt
- ¼ tsp cumin
- ¼ tsp black pepper

- ¼ tspanchochile
- ½ cup salsa
- ½ chopped tomatoes or sauce

How to make it :-

Shredded beef:-

1. Take a slow cooker to begin with and stock at the bottom and put some tomato paste.
2. Place the chuck or pot roast in the slow cooker. And drizzle the spices over it and heat it for five hours.
3. Then take the meat out of the slow cooker and shred the meat with forks or knife.
4. Then we have to separate the fat layer or solid layer from the refrigerated meat juices and use only the liquid part.

Sauce:

1. Take the meat juices and heat it on a stove and put jalapeno, garlic and onions and keep it simmered to

make it soft and to let the excess liquid to get evaporated.

2. Do this for five minutes.
3. Apply salsa and tomato over it, then take it from the heat and stir it till, the point it gets mixed properly.
4. Then pour it over the meat.

Hearty Crock Pot Chili Stew

- Prep time20 mins
- Cook time5 hours
- Total time5 hours 20 mins
- Serves: 12

Ingredients

- 1 lb Ground Beef
- 1 lb Cubed Beef Stew Meat

- 1 28 ounce Can Tomato Puree or Tomato Sauce (one with tomatoes as only ingredient)
- 2 Cups Organic GF Beef Broth or homemade.
- ½ cup pureed pumpkin, or can use ½ cup canned pumpkin puree for thickening.
- 2 Cups Sliced Mushrooms
- 1 Medium Zucchini Squash, chopped
- 1 Medium Onion, Minced
- 6 Cloves Garlic, Minced
- 3 Tbsp Chili Powder
- 1 Tbsp Cumin
- 1 Tsp Garlic Powder
- 2 Tbsp coconut oil or olive oil

How to make it :-

1. First take a big skillet or pan and heat the beef till it gets brown.

2. Then use a crockpot and set the temperature to high.

3. Put tomato puree, beef broth, pumpkin puree, two tablespoon of chili powder, ne teaspoon of garlic powder and one tablespoon of cumin to crock pot and blend it well.

4. Then take one tablespoon of olive oil into the skillet and fry the onions, minced garlic, mushrooms and zucchini squash.

5. Fry till the vegetables become soft.

6. Then put all the vegetable in the slow cooker. In the skillet fry one tablespoon of chili powder, beef stew meat in one tablespoon of olive or coconut oil.

7. Fry till the point the beef becomes brown. Then put the beef stew meat in the slow cooker.

8. Put the lid over it and cook for two to five hours if the temperature is set to low or two hours if it's set to high.

5-Spice Slow-Cooker Pork Ribs

- Prep 2 min.
- Cook 6-12 hours in slow cooker

Ingredients:-

- 3-4 pounds baby back or St. Louis pork ribs
- salt and ground black pepper
- 2 teaspoons Chinese five-spice powder
- 3/4 teaspoon coarse (granulated) garlic powde
- 1 fresh jalapeño, cut into rings
- 2 tablespoons rice vinegar
- 2 tablespoons coconut aminos or homemade substitute
- 1 tablespoon tomato paste

How to make it:

1. Take the ribs and cut into thin pieces.
2. Then place the ribs on a plain surface and put some salt and pepper in it.
3. Then take a small bowl or container and combine Chinese five spices, garlic powder and properly apply it on the meat.
4. Then put the jalapeno on the base of the crockpot and pour rice vinegar, coconut aminos, and tomato paste over it. Blend until the tomato paste has been combined with other items.
5. The put the ribs vertically, and you can put a roasting rack in the crockpot to stop the meat from lying down.
6. Heat for eight to ten hours when the temperature is set to low or for six hours if the temperature is set to high.
7. It is done, when the ribs become soft and then it is time to take it out of the cooker.

8. Put the liquid into a heat- proof container and refrigerate it, till the time the fat separates.
9. Take out the fat and boil the liquid for a few minutes.

   To make the ribs crunchy, heat it at 400 Degrees Fahrenheit.

Easy Barbecue Slow Cooker Ribs

Ingredients:-

- 2 Racks Of Pork Ribs, Cut In Half For 4 Total Segments (Approximately 6-7 Lb Total)
- 1/2 Tbspancho Chili Pepper Powder
- 1/2 Tbsp Chipotle Chili Pepper Powder
- 1/4 Tsp Cinnamon
- 1/4 Tsp Cumin
- Salt And Pepper, To Taste
- 1 Whole White Onion, Sliced

- 6 Cloves Garlic, Crushed
- 1 Tbsp Of Ghee or Fat Of Choice
- 2 C Brian's Barbecue Sauce

How to make it:

1. Switch on the oven and heat it to 400 Degrees Fahrenheit.
2. Take the thin layer out of the lower side of the ribs; it would be like a membrane.
3. Then divide or cut them into two equal pieces. Drizzle some ancho chili pepper, chili pepper, chipotle, cinnamon, cumin and mashed garlic.
4. Also add some pepper and salt.
5. Take a baking sheet and keep it on it and heat it in the oven for fifteen mins.
6. Simultaneously, cut the onions and peel and mash the garlic. Put some ghee, cloves of garlic, and onions in the crockpot.

7. Apply BBQ sauce over the ribs., and put any of the excess sauce on the stacked ribs in the crockpot.

8. Put a lid over the crock pot and heat for six hours and at med-low temperature.

9. After it has been cooked, take it out of the crockpot and keep it aside for the flavors to sink in, then divide it into pieces, or slices.

10. Serve it with additional BBQ sauce if you like.

Slow Cooker Pulled Pork

- Yield: 12 servings

Ingredients:-

For the pulled pork:-

- 3lb boneless pork shoulder (aka. Boston Butt)
- 1 tsp onion powder

- 1 tsp garlic powder
- 1 tsp kosher salt
- 1/2 tsp black pepper
- 1/2 tsp paprika
- 1/2 tsp ground allspice
- 1/2 tsp celery salt
- 1/8 tsp ground cloves
- 1/2 tsp mustard powder
- 1/2 cup water

For the BBQ sauce:-

- 1/2 tsp ground allspice
- 1/4 cup prepared yellow mustard
- 2 tsp hot sauce (I used Frank's Red Hot)
- 3 Tbsp apple cider vinegar
- 3 Tbsp low sugar ketchup
- 4 Tbsp granulated sugar substitute

- 1/2 tsp xanthan gum

How to make it

1. Pulled pork-Take a small bowl or mixing pot and blend all the powdered-garlic, onion, mustard in it.
2. Then also put salt, pepper, paprika, celery salt, cloves and all spices.
3. Blend it properly.
4. Apply the blend over the pork.
5. Then take a slow cooker and put water in it.
6. Then put the readied pork in it.
7. Close the lid and heat for five hours while setting the temperature to high.
8. Heat it till the point it becomes soft and it gets separated.
9. Then take it out, leave some of the juices for later use.
10. And use a knife or a couple of forks for shredding the meat into pieces.

A. Sauce-begin with separating the solid from above the liquid.

B. Then put the items for making the sauce in the slow cooker and stir or blend constantly. And heat it for ten minutes while setting the temperature to high. It's ready to be served hot, when becomes slightly thick.

C. While serving put the meat over the sauce and combine it properly. Tastes best, when served hot!

Slow Cooker Chinese Spare Ribs

- Prep time 20 mins
- Cook time 8 hours
- Total time 8 hours 20 mins
- Serves: 4-6

Ingredients

- 4 lbs pork spare ribs
- 1 tablespoon Chinese five spice
- 1 tablespoon plus 1 teaspoon fresh grated ginger
- 2 teaspoons grated fresh grated garlic
- ¼ cup dry white wine or sherry
- 1 tablespoon plus 1 teaspoon apple cider vinegar
- 2 tablespoons coconut aminos or tamari (I used coconut aminos)
- 1 tablespoon tomato paste
- 1 tablespoon plus 1 teaspoon lemon juice
- optional 2 teaspoons of honey

How to make it

1. First take an oven grill or rack and put it in an oven, and place it a few inches from the direct source of heat.
2. Take a baking foil or sheet and keep a wire rack or grill and put the ribs on it.

3. Then take a small bowl or pot to mix Chinese spices, grated-ginger & garlic.

4. Also put sherry, white wine, apple cider vinegar, tamari, and paste of tomato, lemon juice and some honey.

5. Blend it well. After the broiler is hot enough, put the ribs and keep it under the broiler and cook it till it turns brown on each side.

6. Heat it for four to six minutes.

7. Now take the ribs in a crockpot and put the sauce on the sides of the ribs.

8. Heat the crockpot for around seven to eight hours after putting on the cover.

9. Keep the lid over the crockpot.

10. Enjoy, when it's done!

Conclusion

Thank you again for downloading this book!

I hope this book was able to give you the flavor that you have been looking for in your vitamin water.

The next step is to try the different recipes and share them with the people you hold dear.

Finally, if you enjoyed this book, please take the time to share your thoughts and post a review. It'd be greatly appreciated!

Thank you and good luck!

www.ingramcontent.com/pod-product-compliance
Lightning Source LLC
Chambersburg PA
CBHW071442070526
44578CB00001B/202